William Gerard Don

Memoirs of the Don Family in Angus

With a general survey of the etymology of the name, and of the Scottish family, also, some archaeological appendices

William Gerard Don

Memoirs of the Don Family in Angus
With a general survey of the etymology of the name, and of the Scottish family, also, some archaeological appendices

ISBN/EAN: 9783337240356

Printed in Europe, USA, Canada, Australia, Japan

Cover: Foto ©ninafisch / pixelio.de

More available books at **www.hansebooks.com**

MEMOIRS

OF

THE DON FAMILY IN ANGUS:

WITH

A GENERAL SURVEY OF THE ETYMOLOGY OF THE NAME,

AND OF THE SCOTTISH FAMILY;

ALSO, SOME

ARCHÆOLOGICAL APPENDICES.

BY

WILLIAM GERARD DON, M.D.

DEPUTY   ARMY.

PRINTED FOR PRIVATE CIRCULATION ONLY.

LONDON
1897.

Dedicated

TO

ALL MY RELATIONS, DIRECT OR COLLATERAL, INTERESTED IN THE FAMILY OF DON,

BY

THEIR CLANNISH KINSMAN,

W. G. DON.

52 CANFIELD GARDENS,
    LONDON, N.W.
        May, 1897.

	PAGE
INTRODUCTORY	vii
CHAPTER I.—**The Word Don**	1
I. As A Root	1
II. As A Patronymic	2
CHAPTER II.—**The Family or Clan Don**	5
I. Deuchar's Extracts	7
II. The Baronet's Don	10
III. General Sir George Don, K.C.B.	11
CHAPTER III.—**The Angus Dons**	12
I. Register Records	13
II. Untraced Dons in District	23
CHAPTER IV.—**Genealogical Tables**	24
I. Tables of Descent	25
II. Table of Names	44
III. Table of Occupations	44
CHAPTER V.—**Earlier Dons**	45
I. The Dalbog Dons	46
II. The Forfar and Dundee Dons	49
III. The Blackhall Dons	49
CHAPTER VI.—**The "Botanist" Dons**	53
CHAPTER VII.—**The Brechin Dons**	59
CHAPTER VIII.—**The Bonnyhard Dons**	69
CHAPTER IX.—**The Ballownie Dons**	73

APPENDICES.

I. SCOTTISH SEVENTEENTH CENTURY FARMERS.
II. DAVID SIMPSON'S WILL.
III. THE VALENTINES, LAIRDS OF PITGARVIE, MEARNS.
IV. THE FULLERTONS OF ANGUS AND MEARNS.

INTRODUCTORY.

Y FATHER, **Alexander Don**, third of the name on Ballownie, Stracathro, wrote the first outlines of these Memorials of the Dons in Angus, on the fly-leaves of the Family Bible, in 1847.

At that time he was recovering from a severe accident; including, among other injuries, a broken leg; and in the weary days of convalescence happily bethought him to sketch the Family History.

His genealogies were almost wholly based on oral traditions, collected and treasured up during a long quiet lifetime, spent entirely on natal ground; where, also, for generations, his forefathers had lived and died.

I have heard him express indebtedness, for many early family facts, to Mrs. Rickard, Blackhall; an old lady, of nearly a century back, locally famous for the exercise of a marvellous memory, over the pedigrees of such families as were of long and good standing in the district.

All those interested in these Memorials will be grateful for my father's first sketch; for, had his exceptional knowledge of our earlier genealogy died with him, some interesting portions would have now been beyond recovery, and others proved very difficult to unravel.

Six years after my father's death, and ten after he wrote, I, while a student, corrected and extended his sketch down to 1857.

Twenty years later—in 1875—while quartered in Colchester, I again recast the chronicle, bringing it down to that date.

Once more, in 1897, after another twenty years has passed, and a half-century after my father's time, I essay to rewrite, correct, and greatly extend a fourth, and, as far as I am personally concerned, a final edition, bringing it abreast of the date.

Herein, I have incorporated a great many new family facts; and included an archæological analysis of the etymology of Don, as a word and name; a task which has been rendered possible by the recent great advance in such studies.

I also have given, what my father hardly attempted, brief personal and character sketches, as far as possible, of those of our race who have already passed away ; together with some antiquarian account of the environment of our earlier ancestors.

I have, further, gone behind oral tradition, by a systematic search of the parochial Registers, now in the Register House, Edinburgh, of Stracathro, Brechin, Menmuir, Edzell and Fettercairn, and have been fortunate in not only finding new matter, but bringing accuracy to bear on my father's records.

The information in the Registers still leaves much to be desired ; for these records only begin in the latter part of the sixteenth century ; and during the whole of the seventeenth, and first half of the eighteenth centuries, were most perfunctorily kept ; gaps of months, years, and even decades recur ; then, Births, or rather Baptisms, and Marriages only are recorded : Deaths, never.

But, fortunately, for the purposes of these Memoirs, I have been able to gather from the Registers, as well as other sources, many desired leading records ; which, put together, and reasoned out, sustain the conclusion, that our name and family have existed in the Strathmore Valley for over three centuries, and probably very much longer. There is thus no need to suppose, as my father did, that the Dons only came thence from Aberdeenshire, about the period of the Reformation.

It is obvious a family history once begun, cannot properly be closed, while a survivor remains : and, as the Dons show no signs of exhaustion, or extinction, it is necessary their chronicle should be extended periodically ; but this, as I have found, becomes more and more difficult, in these days of rapid segregation of family units.

Families, in olden times, usually stuck to the limited area, of a few parishes, and there was little difficulty in tracing them ; now, with rapid steam intercommunication, they quickly scatter to the four winds.

The Angus Dons have not escaped such dispersion ; yet, a remnant has been locally left, to keep alive the family traditions, which this history aims at fixing ; and to perpetuate the memory of inter-marriage with many of the old names in the district.

It may not be boasted that the family, in its limited Angus centre ever attained high local position, or wealth ; but, while always in good social repute, and at times graced with members of exceptional culture and intelligence, it, at least, never produced a criminal to tarnish its fair fame.

If, therefore, a 'good name be better than riches,' then the Dons have ever, hitherto, been well endowed; so fully and fairly, indeed, that the most fastidious or censorious existing representative, need not feel, or affect, any reproach, through descent from ancestors, who, if often humble were always honourable; if little distinguished invariably respected; if but simple were ever sterling citizens.

The peculiarity and rarity of the monosyllabic name, and its limited geographical spread, have ever made those who bear it exceptionally clannish; so, that it may truly be said, each Don looks upon every other as a sure and certain kinsman; while cousins many times removed, cherish and cultivate sentiments towards each other, as if of quite near blood relationship.

It has been through such sustained patronymic cohesion, that the family ramifications have been so carefully preserved; and to affectionate interest, strongly transmitted from sire to son, that the Dons can, as very few middle class families are able, recount lineal descent, downwards, from ancestors through three centuries, and eight or ten generations.

The existence of a Family Pedigree, so long, so complete, and so clannish may not be allowed to lapse; and this is my best reason and apology for endeavouring herein to transmit it unbroken to future generations of the name.

I have aimed at making this history as correct and trustworthy as possible; and would fain hope I have succeeded.

But, in order to effect that, I have had to draw on many friends for information; and here acknowledge and thank them all for hearty assistance: especially am I indebted for the valued co-operation of my sister Margaret and brother Alexander; of Mrs. James Don, Mary C. Don, and Anna Ross; of James Don, Brechin; Alexander, Edinburgh; Andrew L., London; George A., Hawkhurst, Kent, and Robert, Davenport, Iowa; also of William Barton and George Memes Low, Edinburgh; and Walter Denham, Glasgow.

W. G. DON.

Chapter I.

THE WORD DON.

HE WORD *DON*, with variations *DAN* and *DUN*, is widely diffused, both in simple and compound forms, in all the Indo-European languages; and may, therefore, be held to have had a primitive central Aryan origin. It has a radical sound, which would naturally suggest itself to the early elaborators of human speech. The word, as it stands, in its root form, and various meaning, will be the first consideration.

I. As a Root.

Is used in two senses; first, as a substantive; secondly, as an adjective.

As a substantive it forms the radical, or primary, in a vast number of ancient place names, of rivers and hills, throughout Europe.

Isaac Taylor, in his wonderful book, *Words and Places*, says: that, in relation to rivers or waters, the root *don* or *dan*, meaning water, is incorporated in the myth of the Danaides; water nymphs, who, in expiation of matrimonial crimes, were condemned to the impossible task of carrying water in leaky urns, to fill a sieve; in which he sees an allegory symbolic of dripping clouds; or perhaps of the readily absorbed waters of the Egyptian inundations. Water, he says, is still simply *don* in the primitive language of the Caucasian tribe of 'Ossetes'; and he detects the original root in Celtic *afon* and *avon*; Gadhelic *tain*; Slavonic *tonn*, all of which are probably derived from the Sanskrit *udan*, water or wet. He points to the fact, that the names of the more important Continental rivers hold the original root: as Don; Danube; Danaster (Dniester); Danasper (Dnieper); Rhodanus (Rhone); Eridanus (Po); etc.: also in Britain: Don; Dean; Dun; Doon; Eden; Devon; Bandon; etc.

He further accounts for the curious intermixture of different radicals for water in the same river names, as follows: When primitive man, in his migrations, came to a notable river, he simply called it the water, or river, in his own language: when other nomadic tribes followed, they adopted the original name without knowing its meaning, but also added their own term for water; thus, after two or three such transformations, the original root became embedded in absurdly tautological compounds; as we now often find it.

But quite apart from its application to rivers, the root *don* or *dun*, as a substantive, also signifies a small and especially a fortified hill. In this sense it enters into a multitude of place names, throughout Britain; especially in Scotland and Ireland; and, although of Celtic origin, is closely cognate to Saxon, *down*, and French *dune*. We have many examples of its use; thus, London (*lyn-don* fortified hill of the marsh); adjective first—substantive last, according to Saxon word combination; as Dundee (*dun-tay*, hill on the river or water); substantive first, adjective last, according to Celtic form.

As an adjective the root, is not applied to rivers or hills; but, in the Celtic spelling *donn*, (so written in the oldest Irish and Scots annals) signifies the colour or quality—brown: and in this sense alone does it enter into personal names and surnames. The word *dun*, a colour, applied specially to animals, is from the same source. I may here mention a curious application of this term; thus: 'donkey,' the familiar and slang name for the ass, is compounded of *don*, and *key*—diminutive; meaning 'the little brown one'; in a similar manner, 'monkey,' in archaic Italian, implies 'the little old woman'!

II. As a Patronymic.

In Celtic the personal name *DON* means the brown-haired or complexioned individual or family (Joyce). It is therefore synonymous with the English name 'Brown'; indeed, so clear has this long been to me, that, when my good friend Robert Barclay Brown was living, I often addressed him as my dear 'Don,' while he returned the joke by calling me his dear 'Brown.'

Consonant with Celtic custom, the original use of adjectives in personal names was merely descriptive; forming nick-names, in fact, distinguishing or discriminating individuals or families, having a common proper name, thus we read of:

Kenneth (III.) 'Donn,' (A.D. 997) the brown Kenneth, in distinction from other King Kenneths; the Gaelic poet, St. Berchan, thus alludes to him:

> 'The 'Donn,' the brown, from strong Duneath' (in Knapdale.)

Donald 'Bane,' (A.D. 1093)—the white or fair Donald; brother to, and usurper after Malcolm Caenmore.

Rhoderick 'Dhu,' the black Roderick, in the 'Lady of the Lake.'

Rob 'Roy,' the red Rob—(Scott).

The Celts did not limit colour nick-names to individuals, or families, but extended them to whole tribes and races; thus, the fierce northern pirates of the eighth and ninth centuries, collectively known as 'Vikings' ('Creekers,' because they operated from inlets on the coast), were distinguished and divided as follows:—

'Finnghaill,' Norse or fair strangers, (from the Celtic roots—*finn* fair, and *gal* stranger).

'Dhubghaill,' Danish or dark strangers, (*dhub* black). (Skene's *Celtic Scotland.*)

It is thus easy to account for the epithet Donn, being extended from individuals to families and tribes; while the variations from the original spelling of the root, are also readily explained on well-known philological principles. No doubt the original spelling *donn*, with a double terminal consonant, better expressed the peculiar Celtic drawl in pronunciation; as did also, another spelling, common two centuries ago, *Done*; both have given way to the shorter, sharper Saxon sound, *Don*. But the change in Ireland is in the vowel; hence *Dunn*; while, it is curious to note the original vowel, nevertheless, is retained in many Irish compound names.; as Donlevy; Donegan; Donnelly; Donovan, etc.

It is only within the last quarter of a century, or so, that the study of place and personal names has been placed on a truly scientific basis; with the result that many older philological views have been dissipated. I can well remember when it was generally taken for granted that the Scottish name Don was derived from the river in Aberdeenshire; but, having my doubts on the matter, I applied, in 1875, to Professor P. W. Joyce of Dublin, the eminent Celtic scholar and antiquary, for his opinion; he favoured me with two most courteous letters, from which are these extracts :—

'Rathgar, Dublin, *11th October, 1875.*'
' . . . Don as it stands is an ancient Celtic term for water, hence its application to rivers is very natural. . After all, your family name may not be from the river. . . . The ancient name Donn, as a personal name, afterwards formed into the family name O'Duinn, now O'Doyne or Doyne, or more commonly Dunn, simply means brown, or brown complexioned, or the brown haired man; of which examples are found in recent times in the two divisions of the O'Conor family . the O'Conor Don (brown) and the O'Conor Roe (red).'

Subsequently, on *16th October, 1875*, he wrote :—

' Our ancient name Donn (which occurs in our oldest records) forms itself several personal and family names; and also enters into combination with other words, and thus goes to form many more names, such as (modern) Donlevy; ancient form 'Donn Sleibhe,' the brown haired chief of the *sleibhe* or mountain, (*sleibhe* pronounced *sleeve*, genitive form *shleibhe* pronounced *levy*); Donnovan ''Donn Dhuban,' the brown haired dark complexioned chief, or person: Donnghal, brown chief of valour (*gal*), whence the family name Donnelly. . . There is a diminutive ending *ran*, usually *gan* in modern language, which forms with Donn, many such names in Ireland as Donegan, Dongan, Dungan; but this particular form will come home to you through Shakespear, Duncan, 'little brown 'man'. Observe where Donn exists both in Ireland and Scotland as a personal and family name, the strong presumption is that all have had the same origin; as the old language of both countries was the same.'

Although Celtic philology has greatly advanced since Professor Joyce wrote the above, I consider his views so absolutely conclusive, then as now, that nothing can be added thereto.

CHAPTER II.

THE FAMILY OR CLAN DON.

PROPOSE under this head to consider the Scottish surname, *DON*, only; although a wider survey would include the rare English form Donne; as well as the more numerous Irish forms, Dunn and Dunne.

I also propose, to limit consideration to the simple root name, and exclude the very numerous compound names, into which, as an essential base it enters; and which raise it to the dimensions of a Clan: these include, Donalds: Donaldsons; Duncans; McDonalds, MacDonnells, etc.

Three leading facts are evident connected with the patronymic Don: first, it is essentially Scottish: secondly, it is strictly limited geographically; lastly, it is very rare.

These points suggest the strong probability that, at some period or place, the family had a common origin, and primary kinship.

There are, of course, Dons scattered throughout the three Kingdoms, and the Colonies: but any I have met, or could trace, always claimed Scottish descent, especially from the mid-east districts.

And, in connection with this latter location it is curious, that a name so essentially Celtic, or Gaelic, should, for centuries and many generations, had its centre in that part of the eastern lowlands which anciently was occupied by the Picts; and further, that, while of Celtic origin, the Dons, as we know or trace them, have always been characteristically Saxon.

I may illustrate the rarity and limitations of the name by the following facts :—

For forty years (with a solitary exception long since wiped out) I have been the sole possessor of the name in the huge and representative Navy, Army and Indian Lists of Officers; which, at any time may number 10,000, and collectively, four or five times that number in four decades. Also, during the past twelve years, while examining medical officer in the great London Recruiting District, I have had the unique experience of inspecting, personally, upwards of 100,000 recruits; yet, in that vast number, only once found a man bearing my own name; he, unfortunately, could tell me nothing of his forebears, beyond that his father belonged to London.

In the great representative Directories of London, Liverpool, Manchester and Glasgow, only a mere handful of Dons are found; and these are either our own relations, or presumedly Scottish.

After considerable investigation I place the old Scottish centres of the Dons in the following order of priority:

    East Perthshire.
    Angus.
    Stirling.
    Berwick.
    Edinburgh.
    Moray.

I also trace families in Lanark, Ayr and Dumbarton, but consider them recent migrations.

The family I had long noticed in Kent, are, I am glad recently to find, descendants of George Don, the 'Forfar Botanist.'

The above localization of the name is fully borne out in a curious manuscript, compiled from legal sources, which my cousin, the Honorable David Don, of Natal, purchased in Edinburgh, and presented to me. This interesting, and, although fragmentary, really valuable work, is entitled: *Genealogical Collection, relative to the Family of Don*, collected by Alex. Deuchar, Genealogist, Edinburgh. It bears no date, but, from the quality of the paper, and style of penmanship, affords material evidence of being at least a hundred years old; it was one of many such collections made by the eccentric Deuchar; who is described as 'Seal Engraver to His Majesty (probably George III.) and Genealogist.'

Deuchar's method was to extract notices of Families from such legal records, as, *General Register of Sasines, Commissariot Testaments, Law Cases, Parochial Registers*, etc.

Attached to his *Don Search* are blank sheets, headed 'List of Records Searched'; 'See Notices of this Family in Nesbit'; 'See Genealogy in Playfair, Vol. 8'; 'Don Printed Great Seal'; 'Note of Pages and No. where this Family occurs. Nil.'

I have not been able to consult these references, but the final word 'Nil,' does not encourage research. Deuchar's manuscript extracts, are sometimes difficult to decipher, not merely from cramped penmanship but tantalizing legal contractions; while those in print being in legal dog-Latin, are hard to translate; but, in case of the ultimate loss of this curious document, I transcribe it carefully as it stands, adding some notes.

I.—Deuchar's Extracts.

'Edinburgh Commissariot Testamentary Records.'
'Alexander Don, Chapman, Fettercarden, Kincardine, Mearns, '29th Novr. 1608.'
NOTE.—This proves the existence of a Fettercairn packman of the name in the latter part of the sixteenth century; he was doubtless a relation, but whether an ancestor of the Angus Dons cannot be stated. The date is probably that of the proving of the will; but why that happened in Edinburgh does not transpire.

'Marion Done, Edr., Da. of Decd., John D. in Frew, 3 August '1653.'
NOTE.—Observe spelling of 'Done.' Frew, near Kippen, Stirling. The Dons of Teath, or Teith, were an old county family in that neighbourhood.

'Register of Deeds; McKenzie Office.'
'25 Octr. 1711. B. Thos. Scott, to John Done of Auldtenburn.'
NOTE.—Evidently Attonburn, in Roxburgh, of which a John Done was proprietor in 1696.

'17 Octr. 1711. Thos. Done, Nr., Elgin, To, Ludovick Brodie, of Whitefield.'
NOTE.—This is a record of Dons in Morayshire.

'3 July 1711. Prot. Wm. Don, Vintor, Edr.'
NOTE.—Perhaps a Vintner in Edinburgh.

'20 Dec. 1711. Sir Alexander Don of Rutherford, and other 'Dons.'
NOTE.—As explained, under the Baronets, this Sir Alexander was a Knight, of Rutherford, Roxburgh; and second son of the first Baronet, Sir Alexander, of Newton, Berwick.

'*Commissariote of Lauder Tests.*'

' 18 March 1697, Sir Alex. Don of Newton, 2nd Esk, 26 July
' 1692, Sir Alex. Don of Newton x Sir James D. of Newton.'

NOTE.—Sir James succeeded his father as second Baronet ; see observations under Baronets.

'*Edinburgh Commissariote Testaments.*'

'30 June 1582, Janet Ductor Sp., John Done in Hillock of
' Tillyforgan, Banachy Parish.'

NOTE.—I fail to identify these places ; but believe them to be in Perthshire ; the word ' in ' shows that John was tenant in Hillock of Tillyforgan. ' Ductor ' is probably a legal phrase, and not part of the wife Janet's name.

'*Dunblane Commissariote Testaments.*'

' 11 July 1598, John Done x 1596 per John (mover) in Inch *ret*
"*pav fowllis* by Gilbt. Don for himself and childr. of Defunct.'

NOTE.—This was probably the same John Done as the foregoing, but the contractions are enigmatical.

' 15 Oct. 1543, Cater Don Exr. John and Alex. Gilfillan nr.
' L ——— s.'

NOTE.—This is the earliest of Deuchar's Extracts, and is also enigmatical.

' 10 Feby. 1553, Sir David Don, Robt. and John Done.'

NOTE.—Showing there were Dons of title in the sixteenth century, probably connected with the Teath family.

' 1 April 1601, Patr. Don in Doun x 1600 by Himself. John,
' Margarie, Margt. Mitchell only Ex John Hadden Wit.'

' Jas. Done servitor to Earl Morray, and Jas. and Alex. . . .
' overseers sd. Jas. Done, Cautioner Confr. . . . by Dept. to
' John Hadden his son-in-law Gilbt. Thomson and Isabella
' Werketurn his Sp. To Alex. Don son of James supr.'

NOTE.—This is very obscure as to persons, places and legal facts ; James was apparently a sort of factor to Earl Morray, and had as overseers, relatives named James and Alexander.

' 25 Augst. 1618, Kath. Oliphant Sp. of James Done in Finden-
' gask x 1614 by Jas. for John Don and his son Pat Don in Innes,
' during Bn. of James Caitn.'

NOTE.—Findengask, or Findogask, Perthshire ; this confirms tradition mentioned by George A. Don of Hawkhurst, Kent, of intermarriage between the Dons and Oliphants of Gask. The Pat Don, in Innes, was probably son of John, previously mentioned, in Inch; Innes and Inch—Gaelic for island—being the same.

'9 Sep. 1620. Berleance Don—John Don in Frew x 1618, 'Helen, Marion, Margt., Marjory, Jean.'

NOTE.—This apparently refers to the daughters of John Don in Frew, a man who seems to have been troubled with much litigation.

'*Partn. Register Sasines Peebles.*'

'Sas. Sir James Don, of Newton, A.R., 16 Dec. 1692.'

NOTE.—Compare Lauder Commissariot.

'*Edinburgh Commissariote Testaments.*'

'1 May 1734, Jas. Don of Woodside.'

'7 July 1737, Mayr. Thomas Don, Scotts fuzillens.'

NOTE.—Woodside unknown. Thomas seems to have been a Major in the Scots Fusiliers?

The foregoing extracts are in manuscript; the following are printed, in legal Latin, which I translate to the best of my ability :—

'EDINBURGH.'

'1249. Jul 13, 1678, Elizabeth and Maria Don, joint heiresses 'of their grandfather, Alexander Don, tailor in Edinburgh, avi in 'tenement in Edinburgh. E 3s 4d, xxxiv. 37.'

'INQUISITIONES GENERALES.'

'5523. Maii 7, 1672. Lord (or Sir) Alexander Don of Newton, 'soldier Baronet, heir of Patrick Don, Writer to the Royal Signet, son 'of his Uncle, xxxi., 52, 7746. Jul 27, 1696, John Don of Attonburne, 'heir of his Father, Master Patrick Don, of Attonburne, xlvi., 310.'

'ROXBURGH.'

'316. July 27, 1696. John Don of Attonburne, heir of 'Master Patrick Don of Attonburne, his Father, in the lands and 'house of Attonburne, from the east and west sides of the same, 'with the appurtenance called Cove, below the parish of Mow, and 'now by annexation below the parish of Morebattle, with the tenth '*gurbalibus* (tiends?) for the rector and vicar from the heads A E '£10, N E £15, land and barony of Plenderleith A E £10, 'N E £60, *in warrantum* of the lands of Attonburne, ect.'

NOTE.—The first of these extracts refers to a successful Knight of the Thimble in Edinburgh; the two last, to the Dons from whom sprang the Baronets.

II. The Baronets DON.

The historic facts connected with the Baronets are these :

Alexander Don of Newton, Berwickshire, now Newton Don, was a baronet of the Restoration, created 7th June, 1667 ; who, through an Edinburgh Writer to the Signet, was probably descended from the Dons of Teith. He had three sons : (1) **James**, who succeeded in the baronetcy ; (2) **Alexander** of Rutherford, Roxburgh, who was knighted ; and (3) **Patrick**, who married Ann, daughter and heiress of Sir John Wauchope, Senator of the College of Justice, of Edmonstone, Midlothian ; by whom he had two sons, **John** and **James** ; who assumed their maternal name Wauchope. After eight baronets Don had passed, the last being **Sir William Henry Don**, notorious as an actor, ect., the baronetcy, in default of male heirs, passed to John, descendant of James Wauchope, who assumed the name Sir John Don-Wauchope as ninth baronet. The estate of Newton Don went to Mr. Balfour, who is now proprietor. The Baronet Don crest is a pomegranate with the motto, 'Non deerit alter aureus,' which may be translated, 'Another golden one will not be wanting' ; a somewhat obscure allusion, but may have a recondite reference to the mythical Hesperidean Nymphs, who kept the garden with the golden apples (oranges or pomegranates) of Hera.

My cousin, Walter Denham, himself an accomplished genealogist, sends me the following extract from '**Norman People**,' page 228 ; which I transcribe, not because I attach much value to it, but in order to comment on the supposed origin of the Baronets Don.

'DON, Richereld tu Don, Normandy 1180-95 (M.R.S). Hence 'the Baronets Don.'

'Don, from Dune, Normandy, Ralph and Hervey de Duna of 'Normandy; Richard de Duna William and Robert 1165, held 'several Knights Fees in Devon, Cornwall and Derby (Lig. Nig.) 'Henry de Dona occurs in Essex (Mon ii 954); William occurs in 'Normandy (M.R.S.)'

The above are no doubt accurate extracts from trustworthy records ; but the inference 'hence the Baronets Don,' is, to the archæologist, sheer nonsense. They only show that there were ancient as there probably are modern Norman Dons; for, I have already pointed out that the Celtic roots—*don* water, and *dun* or *dune* hill, are common in place names of Northern France; so that, Richard de Duna, and Henry de Dona, respectively, mean nothing more than Richard of the Hill, and Henry of the River. The Baronets' name, Don, is from other sources entirely, and existed in Britain and Ireland many centuries before the Normans were heard of. The truth is, competent archæologists view all heraldic pedigrees with distrust; more especially those in which the Norman cult or craze comes in; for, the makers of such (to order) simply draw largely on their imaginations, with one object only, to prove that all men worthy of being ennobled must necessarily have had a Norman origin !

III. General Sir George DON. K.C.B.

A distinguished officer of his day, and Colonel of the 36th Regiment. I am not certain, but think it probable he belonged to the Forfar Dons, from an incident which will be mentioned in the life of the Forfar Botanist. He was apparently born about 1760: and in 1804 was Governor of Jersey, then of great strategic importance, in the war with France. I have a fine portrait of him in full uniform as Governor; he made nearly all the existing roads, and forts in Jersey; for, although an infantry soldier, he was a very capable engineer; several streets in St. Heliers are named after him; and the Jersey States in 1880 erected a handsome statue to his memory.

Afterwards, he was Governor of Gibraltar, where he died in 1832, and was buried in the Cathedral there. By permission of the Spanish Government, with whom he was a great favorite, he built a paved road, which still more or less exists, to San Roque, where he had a Villa, and was allowed to reside.

When quartered in Gibraltar, in 1878, I met old people who knew Sir George; notably the ex-Chief Justice, Sir James Cochrane, who resided there; and who showed me much kindness as one bearing the name of Don, declaring I had a distinct family likeness to his old friend and patron !

Chapter III.

THE ANGUS DONS.

AVING briefly discussed, in general terms, the Name and Family, or Clan, I now come to the specific branch of the Dons with which these Memoirs are immediately concerned. I have already stated that the Dons have existed in North Angus and South Mearns for at least three centuries; and probably much longer. They were originally confined there to a very limited area, scarcely exceeding a radius of seven miles from a central point in Stracathro; and lived chiefly in the parishes of Stracathro, Brechin, Edzell, Menmuir and Fettercairn; also perhaps Logie Pert and Dun.

In view of these facts I caused the old Registers of the five parishes first named, now in the Register House, Edinburgh, to be searched: and all the entries under Don extracted. This important duty was faithfully discharged by my cousin, Alexander Don, of the Royal Bank of Scotland, Edinburgh; who, partly himself, but chiefly through a professional searcher (Rev. Mr. McLeod), had the work thoroughly done.

The initial misfortune here is, that the Registers do not go sufficiently far back; for there seems to have been no system of pre-Reformation registration. The oldest of them available are those of Brechin, beginning in 1612; but one and all are imperfect; only Baptisms and Marriages are recorded, not Deaths. Even the best of them had been most perfunctorily kept, having blanks of months, years and sometimes decades; while the entries made are occasionally difficult to understand. These irregularities and imperfections during the whole of the seventeenth and part of the eighteenth centuries are of course mainly explained by the see-saw of political and religious revolution then going on. The information afforded for the purpose of this Memoir if, seldom consecutive or complete, is, however, on the whole, fairly satisfactory; the search having disclosed new and cleared up old facts; and, settled once for all, the full possible extent of the family history to be gathered from the parochial Registers. The early history of the Family is now therefore no longer merely based on oral tradition.

1. Register Records.

The following Registers were searched :—

I. *Brechin.*
   (1) Marriages, 1700 to 1819, Vol. I.
   (2) Baptisms, 1612 to 1753, Vols. I. to III.

II. *Stracathro.*
   (1) Marriages, 1709 to 1820.
   (2) Baptisms, 1709 to 1819.

III. *Menmuir.*
   (1) Marriages, 1705 to 1782.
   (2) Baptisms, 1707 to 1777.

IV. *Edzell.*
   (1) Marriages, 1641 to 1820.
   (2) Baptisms, 1684 to 1703.

V. *Fettercairn.*
   (1) Marriages, 1669 to 1744.
   (2) Baptisms, 1721 to 1730.

The following extracts were made, literally, with notes in brackets, by the searcher.

1. *Brechin Marriages.* 1700 to 1819. (Searched to 1704, then blank to June 1720)

(1) 1722. June 1. **James Don** in the parish of Caraldstone and **Margaret Langlands** in this parish were matrimonially contracted, and married June 22. (Half of a leaf torn away, 1727-8 ; blank, May 1728 to April 1743.)

(2) 1745. Jany. 12. **Alexander Don**, in Mains of Ballewney, in the parish of Strickathrow, and **Janet Prophet**, servitrix to John Mollison, one of the present Baillies of Brechin, in this parish, were matrimonially contracted and married Feby. 8. (See Table III.)

(3) 1747. April 30. **Alexander Smith** in Pitpollux, and **Janet Done** there, were matrimonially contracted and married. (See Table III, and correction.)

(4) 1762. July 20. **James Smith** in this parish, and **Jean Don** in the parish of Rescobie, were contracted.

(5) 1768. Sep. 23. **Thomas Don** and **Janet McKenzie** both in this parish were matrimonially contracted. (See Table V.)

(6) 1769. May 12. **George Allan** and **Jean Don** both in this parish were matrimonially contracted.

(7) 1780. Feb. 18. **Thomas Strachan** and **Helen Don** both in this parish were matrimonially contracted.

(8) 1787. July 6. **James Rheny**, Wright in Brechin, and **Isabel Don** there, Daur. of Thomas Don, farmer in the parish of Strickmartin (Strathmartin?) were contracted in order to marriage, and having been proclaimed three several Sabbaths and no objection offered were married the 27th of said month of July.

(9) 1790. Feby. 12. **David Mowat**, widower, Weaver in Brechin, and **Margaret Don** in Upper Tenements were contracted in order to marriage, and having been proclaimed three several times, and no objections offered were married the 15th curt.

(10) 1797. June 9. **Thomas Don**, Wright in Brechin, and **Jean Barclay** in the parish of Montrose, were contracted in order to marriage, and their Banns having been published three several times and no objection offered were married the 16th day of said June. (See Table V.)

(11) 1800. Sep. 19. **James Don**, Hammerman in Brechin, and **Mary Carnegie** there, Daur. of the deceased William Carnegie, in Pous, were contracted in order to marriage, and their Banns having been published three several times and no objection offered were married 27th day of said month. (See Table VII.)

(Searched to this date.)

NOTE. -Of the above marriages only Nos. 2, 3, 5, 10 and 11 can be identified as belonging to this Memoir.

II. *Brechin Baptisms.* 1612 to 1671. Vol. I.

(1) 1641. May 23. **James Don** spous to **Jean Cramond** had a man child baptized named **Alexander**. Wit: Alex: Kid; Alex: Cramond; Alex: Don.

(2) 1655. July 4. **James Don**, in Airdo, husband to **Margaret Cramond**, had a maid child baptized named **Magdalen**. Wit: Alex: Mather, David Mill Younger and Elder.

(3) 1657. Dec. 16. **James Don** husband to **Jean Cramond** had a man child baptized named **Alexander**. Wit: Alex: Fairweather; Alex: Henry; Alex: Don.

NOTE.—The two James Don's here mentioned, were perhaps cousins, married to sisters, named Cramond. Airdo farm is in Stracathro.

1672 to 1725. VOL. II.

(4) 1672. Dec. 1. **Alexander Don** husband to **Isobel Erskin** had a maid child baptized named **Marat.** (*sic*) Wit: Mr. James Nicholson, Alex: Mather and John Bellie.

(5) 1681. Dec. 4. **Alexander Don** husband to **Isabell Erskyn** had a maid child bapt. named **Helin**. Wit: John Mathie; John Gain and John Mather.

(6) 1684. Oct. 30. **Arthure Don** husband to **Katheren Dees** had a maid child bapt. **Janet**. Wit: Will Kinnear; Alex: Brews.

(7) 1686. June 27. **Arthure Don** husband to **Katharen Deass** had a maid child bapt. **Margaret**. John Stenison, Tho. Wallentine, James Deass, Witnesses.

(Vol. III. 1725 to 1753, searched to Dec. 1743, but no more entries of Don found).

NOTE.—I cannot identify any of these extracts. The two James's being contemporaries of Thomas of Dalbog make it not improbable that James of Airdo was Thomas's brother; and consequently a son of Alexander of Stracathro. (See No. 1. Edzell Marriages). The name Arthur also occurs among the Menmuir Dons, and suggests at least cousinship. Observe the uncertain spelling of the names of Alexander's and Arthure's wives; variations characteristic of the wayward orthography of the seventeenth century.

I. *Stracathro Marriages.* 1709 to 1819.

(Searched from 1709 to 1715; then Register wanting till 1764.)

(1) 1773. **Robert Galdie** and **Jean Don** both in this parish after their Banns of marriage were orderly published, were married here January the 1st day. (See Table III.)

(2) 1775. **Alexander Stoole** and **Kathren Don** in this parish both, after their Banns of marriage were orderly published were married here July the 8th day. (See Table III.)

(3) 1775. **Alexander Don** and **Jean Hood** both in this parish after their Banns of marriage were orderly published were married here upon the 8th day of Decr. (See Table XI.)

(4) 1788. **William Hood** and **Christian Don** both in this parish after their Banns of Marriage were orderly published were married here upon the 12th day of July. (See Table III.)

(5) 1798. **David Webster** of the parish of Menmuir, and **Jean Don**, of this parish, of Strickathrow were married the 10th November 1798, after their Banns were published. (See Table XI.)

(6) 1807. **David Don** of the parish of Edzell, and **Christian Hood** of this parish, were married upon the 16th June 1807, after their Banns were regularly published. (See Table VI. Compare Edzell Marriage 12.)

(7) 1820. **Alexander Don** of this parish and **Jean Fullerton** of the parish of Brechin were married on the 22nd July 1820. (See Table XII.)

NOTE.—All of the above seven marriages are duly accounted for in the text of these Memoirs.

II. *Stracathro Baptisms.* 1709 to 1819. (Original Register searched to 1819; but a duplicate in modern handwriting not searched.)

NOTE.- ·The duplicate probably written by the Rev. Wm. Gerard.

1. 1746. **Alexander Don** lawful son to **Alexander Don** in Ballownie was baptized on the 15th day of September. (This is twice entered in the Register.) (See Tables III. and XI.)

(2) 1748. **Cathren Don**, daughter to **Alexander Don** and **Janet Prophet** in Ballownie was baptized May 29th.

(3) 1751. **Alexander Don** in Ballownie had a daughter baptized January 25th called **Jean**.

(Register defective ; very few entries 1752-55).

(4) 1777. **Jean Don**, lawful daughter to **Alexander Don** and **Jean Hood**, his spouse, in Ballownie, was born January 7th and baptized the 9th of said month. (See Table XI.)

(5) 1778. **Jannet Don**, lawful daughter to **Alexander Don** and **Jean Hood**, his spouse, in Ballownie, was born upon the 11th day of August, and Baptized upon the 14th of said month.

(6) 1781. **John Don,** lawful son to **Alexander Don** and **Jean Hood** his spouse, in Ballownie was born upon the 3rd day of March, and Baptized upon the 5th day of said month.

(7) 1782. **Alexr.** ~~John~~ (*sic*) lawful son to **Alexander Don** and **Jean Hood** his spouse in Ballownie was Born upon the 19th day of November, and Baptized upon the 24th day of said month.

NOTE.—The above curious correction in the birth and baptism of my father exists in the Register.

(8) 1782. **Charles Don** lawful son to **Thomas Don** at Inchbear, and his spouse **Janet** ~~Margaret~~ (sic) **McKenzie** was born upon the 19th day of December and Baptized the 29th of said month. (See Table V.)

NOTE.—This was one of the seven sons of Thomas of Brechin and Dunninald ; how he came to be born at Inchbare, close to Ballownie, I do not know.

(9) 1784. **David Don** lawful son to **Alexander Don** and **Jean Hood**, his spouse, was Born upon the 5th day of July, and Bapt. on the 8th of said month.

(10) 1786. **George Don** lawful **son** ~~daughter~~ (*sic*) to **Thomas Don** at Ballownie and **Margaret McKenzie** his spouse was Born upon the 5th day of April and Baptized the 9th of said month. (See Table V.)

NOTE.—This was the seventh and youngest son of Thomas of Brechin, who was apparently born while his mother was on a visit to Ballownie.

(11) 1786. **Mary Don** lawful daughter to **Alexander Don** and his spouse was Born upon the 23rd day of May and Baptized upon the 28th of said month—parents living in Ballownie.

(12) 1788. **Robert Don,** lawful son to **Alexander Don** and **Jean Hood** his spouse in Ballownie was Born upon the 5th day of February and Baptized the 13th of said month.

(13) 1790. **Thomas Don,** lawful son to **Alexander Don** and **Jean Hood** his spouse was born on the 11th April and baptized the 25th of said month 1790.

(14) 1791. **William Don,** lawful son to **Alexander Don** and **Jean Hood** in Ballownie, was born July 1st and Baptized the 12th day of said month, 1791.

(15) 1793. **Hannah Don** lawful Daur. to **Alexander Don** and **Jean Hood** in Ballownie, was born October 22nd and baptized Novr. 2nd 1793.

(16) 1795. **James Don**, lawful son to **Alexander Don** and **Jean Hood** in Ballownie, was born Decr. 10th and bapt. Decr. 26th. (Entry partly torn away.)

(17) 1798. **James Don** lawful son to **Alexander Don** and **Jean Hood** was born at Ballownie the 10th Sepr. and bapt. on the 27th Sepr., 1798.

(Searched original Register to 1819, but duplicate in modern handwriting not searched.)

NOTE.—All the above 17 records are duly noted in the text of these Memoirs.

The early Stracathro Registers of the seventeenth century appear to have been destroyed; although those of the same period in the adjoining parishes are preserved; if, however, in an imperfect condition.

I. *Menmuir Marriages.* 1704 to 1782.

(Prior to 1766 the entries are few, and mixed up with other matters).

(1) 1705. January 21. **John Gald** with **Margaret Don** were married here on the second of January 1705, after contract and proclamatione according to order. (See Table II.)

(2) 1706. Decr. 1. This day **James Don** was chosen Collector for the following year.

NOTE.—Collector of Kirk Session Funds.

(Register searched 1704 to 1782; no further record till 1848.)

II. *Menmuir Baptisms.* 1707 to 1777.

(1) 1707. May 12. **Charles Don** had a child baptized, and called his name **John**. (See Table II).

(2) 1707. Aug. 2. **James Don**, Younger in Blackhall, had a child baptized named **Jannet**. (See Table II.)

(3) 1715. July 13. **James Don** Yr. in Blackhall had a daughter baptized named **Isobel**.

(4) 1717. April 28. This day **James Don**, in Blackhall had a son baptized named **Alexander**.

NOTE.—The term "Younger" is here omitted, but clearly implied; the gap in the Register between 1707 and 1715 was no doubt from faulty registration or perhaps loss of Register.

(5) 1719. Feby. 8. **James Don**, Younger in Blackhall, had a child baptized named **Margaret**.

(6) 1721. March 5. This day **James Don**, Younger in Blackhall had a child baptized named **Catherine**.

(7) 1721. July 19. **Arthur Don** in Muirside of Balzeordie had a child baptized named **Anna**. (See Table II.)

(8) 1723. January 27. **Arthur Don**, in Damhead, had a child baptized named **John**.

(9) 1723. Decr. 1. **James Don**, Younger in Blackhall, had a child baptized named **James**.

NOTE.—Charles, James (Younger) and Arthur were evidently sons of James (senior) of Blackhall; by his first wife Isobel Fairweather.

(10) 1725. July 11. **Alexander Don**, in Blackhall, had a child baptized named **Thomas**. (See Table III.)

NOTE.—This Alexander, son of James (senior) in Blackhall and his (second) wife, Isobel Fyfe, was born in 1700, and succeeded to the farm on his father's death 1724. He was half-brother of Charles, James (younger), and Arthur. He soon removed to Ireland, and ultimately to Ballownie.

(11) 1725. Aug. 11. **Arthur Don**, in Damhead, had a child baptized named **Margaret**.

(12) 1726. Oct. 12. **Alexander Don**, in Blackhall, had a child baptized named **Isobel**.

NOTE.—This daughter had the romantic history—afterwards detailed.

(13) 1728. Oct. 23. **Alexander Don** in Ireland had a son baptized called **James**.

NOTE.—Alexander had now removed from Blackhall to Ireland.

(14) 1728. Nov. 24. **James Don**, in Blackhall, had a daughter baptized named **Jean**.

NOTE.—James, not now termed younger, his father having died in 1724. The tenancies of Blackhall and Mill of Blackhall were evidently mixed up in the Registers; James, younger, was, I fancy, the "Miller"; he, at all events, remained at Blackhall, after his brother Alexander had removed to Ireland.

(15) 1733. March 11. **Alexander Don** in Ireland, had a son baptized called **David**. (See Table III.)

NOTE.—This David was progenitor of the Bonnyhard Dons.

(16) 1762. Sep. 8. **Alexander Don** in Ireland had a daughter baptized named **Jean**. (See Table IV.)

NOTE.—This Alexander was son of James (younger) born in 1717, baptisms No. 4; he apparently remained for a time at Ireland, after his uncle Alexander's removal to Ballownie, which took place in 1742.

(17) 1764. Oct. 11. **Alexander Don** had a son baptized named **George**.

NOTE.—This George was afterwards famous as the Forfar Botanist.

(18) 1766. March 1. **Alexander Don** had a son baptized named **William**.

(19) 1768. Nov. 11. **Alexander Don** had a daughter baptized named **Margaret**.

(20) 1772. Sep. 7. **Alexander Don**, in Muirton of Balzeordie had a daughter baptized named **Isobel**.

(21) 1774. July 5. **Alexander Don**, in Balzcordie, had a daughter baptized named **Jannet**.

(22) 1777. Dec. 13. **Alexander Don** in Meadow Burnhead had a daughter baptized named **Anna**.

NOTE.—Alexander evidently moved twice between 1762 and 1777.

I. *Edzell Marriages.* 1641 to 1703. Vol. I. (Intermixed with other matters.)

(1) 1647. November. On the first day a marriage was contracted with **Thomas Don** in the parish of Strickathrow, and **Agnes Stewart** in this Parish. Cautioner for the man **Alexander Don**, his father, and for the woman Wm. Guthrie. (See Table I).

NOTE.—This is the most important of all these extracts. From the Couple here united descended the Angus Dons recorded in these Memoirs. This notice is all we know of the seventeenth century Alexander of Strickathrow. He was probably a farmer (perhaps in Ballownie?) and no doubt nearly related to the contemporary Dons in Airdo, Brechin and Fettercairn.

(Register blank Sep. 1662 to Sep. 1664).

(2) 1665. November 8. **Alexander Grieg**, in Aberlemno, with **Agnes Don** in this parish for the first tyme; 1665. Decr. 3. Alexander Grieg with Agnes Don for the second tyme. The same day Alexander Grieg in Aberlemno with Agnes Don were proclaimed for the third tyme. (See Table I.)

(3) 1666. July. **Thomas Don** in the Mill of Dalbogue appointed an Elder.

(Register blank Aug. 1652 to Oct. 1665; Jany. 1680 to July 1684).

(4) 1696. July 24. **David Low** and **Margaret Don** was lawfullie maryed and proclaimed.

(5) 1703. Aug. 10. **Thomas Jollie** and **Jean Don** were married.

(Searched to August 1703, then blank to Jany. 1715)—Vol. II. Register 1715 to 1820.

(6) 1760. July 19. **David Done** in the parish of Strickathrow and **Jean Henderson** in this parish were contracted together in order to marriage.

NOTE.—The origin of the Bonnyhard Dons (compare Menmuir Baptism No. 15. See Table VI).

(7) 1785. August 1. **Alexander Don** and **Agnes Smart**, both in this parish, contracted together in order to marriage.

NOTE.—This Alexander, farmer in Priestown, was son of David and Jean Henderson in Bonnyhard.

(8) 1788. January 26. **Alexander Duncan** and **Elizabeth Done**, both in this parish, contracted together in order to marriage.

(9) 1789. June 6. **David Fettes** in this parish and **Jean Don** in the parish of Strickathrow, were contracted together in order to marriage. (See Table III. and compare Stracathro Baptisms No. 3.)

(Register blank Jany. 1791 to Dec. 1804).

(10) 1805. June 22. **John Anderson** in the parish of Marykirk, and **Margaret Don** in this parish were contracted in order to marriage. (See Table VI.)

(11) 1807. March 21. **Robert Watson** and **Ann Don**, both in this parish, were contracted together in order to marriage.

(12) 1807. June 13. **David Don** in this parish, and **Christian Hood** in parish of Strickathrow, were contracted together in order

to marriage. (See Table VI, and compare Stracathro Marriages No. 6.)

(13.) 1817. Sep. 13. **John Smith**, tenant in Dalfouper, and **Jean Don** residing at Hole of Slateford, both in this parish, were contracted together in order to marriage, and they were married on the 20th day of the said month of September.

(Searched to 22nd April 1820).

II. *Edzell Baptisms.* 1684 to 1703. (Intermixed with other matters.)

(1) 1684. Upon the 25 day of October **John Don** had a chyld baptized her name **Jean**, before John Donaldson in Bonhard, and David Will in Cowiehill. (See Table I.)

NOTE.—This John was eldest son of Thomas and Agnes Stewart in Dalbog, in which farm he succeeded his father in 1672; there is no record of his birth, marriage or marriages; but my father mentions he had twenty-one children! Nine of them are here recorded; some of his sons were progenitors of the Dons in Forfar and Dundee.

(2) 1686. April 2. **John Don** in Dalbog had a chyld baptized, his name **Robert**, before Francis Nicoll in Shanon, and James Duncan in Cornefearne.

(3) 1688. March 19. **John Don** had a daughter baptized her name **Jannett**, before James Duncan and Francis Nicoll.

(4) 1690. Bapt. **Alexander Don**, son to **John Don** Wednesday 8 January, befor Mr. John Lindsay and George Will.

(5) 1691. Dec. 4. **John Don** had ane child baptized his name **David**, before these Witnesses, David Ogilvie and David Will.

(6) 1694. Jany. 12. **John Don** had ane child baptized hir name was **Elspet**, before these Witnesses, Andrew Lyell and Walter Lindsay.

(7) 1695. December 5. **John Don** had ane child baptized hir name was **Anne**. Wit. David Ogilvie and David Will.

NOTE.—This name altered but more like Anne than anything else. **Ane** on margin. The Registrar at this period evidently a poor scholar!

(8) 1697. July 26. **John Don** had ane child baptized his name is **Thomas**, before these Witnesses, Thomas Low, and Thomas Alexander.

(9) 1701. June 9. **John Don** had ane child baptized her name is **Ane** (*sic*) before these Witnesses, James Duncan and Walter Lindsay.
NOTE.—The previous 'Ane' had evidently died in childhood. (Searched to Sep. 1703 then blank till March 1715).

I. *Fettercairn Marriages.* 1669 to 1744.
(Searched to 1675, then blank to 1721, and afterwards mixed up with Baptisms ect: searched to 2nd January 1730, no entries of Don).

II. **Untraced Dons in District.**

In the eight or ten parishes grouped around Stracathro, and also further afield in north Angus and south Mearns, there are a few Dons to be found, whose direct relationship to our family cannot be traced. But although not identified, there can be little doubt they all sprang from the same stock originally; for the name is much too rare and circumscribed to permit of any other conclusion.

Among the untraced Dons, now living is James Don, Blacksmith, Chapelton; a sturdy, intelligent man of eighty years, who had a large family. He informed me that he was born in Farnell, and thought his ancestors came rather from the Forfar, than the Brechin direction, but did not really know. If from Forfar he may be descended from the Rescobie Don, mentioned in Brechin Marriages No. 4.

Hercules Don, a man of ninety years, now living at Whitefield of Dun, I am informed, considers himself related to the above James Don, but claims Brechin descent—possibly from some of the unknown Dons mentioned in the early Brechin Register. This old man also speaks of a Don and his wife, interred in Pert, Churchyard, but who had no gravestone; these people may have been connected with, or even descended from the original Alexander, in the adjoining parish of Stracathro, during the seventeenth century.

It is quite evident, from all of the foregoing, that, the name and family of Don having been fairly numerous in the Brechin District, early in the seventeenth century, must have existed there long previously. They may, indeed, be a Celtic survival from a time before the era of David I, and the Battle of Stracathro, in 1130, after which came the Anglo-Saxon settlement of these lowlands. In Saxon speech, the Celtic adjective and affix Donn, would naturally assume substantive form, and so develop into a proper surname. With such vitality in the past, long may the Family flourish in the future!

Chapter IV.

GENEALOGICAL TABLES.

FROM parish Registers, and many Family Records, I have been able to construct Twelve Tables; which, as far as known, trace out the Family Pedigree, from about 1590 to the present date—1897.

Every endeavour has been made to record names and dates correctly; although some of the latter can only be given approximately.

Sons are traced in direct descent; and Daughters' Husbands, and their children down in the first generation, as far as information is available.

Cross references, both in the Tables and Text, will afford facility for tracing Pedigree ramifications.

Two supplementary Tables are appended: the first showing the relative frequency of Male and Female Christian names of Dons in the Pedigree Tables; where there are two or more such names, the first only is given, except in recognized compound female names such as Mary Ann; the second abstract shows the Occupations of the Dons, and of daughters' husbands and sons, grouped under the usual Census headings.

I.—TABLES OF DESCENT.

TABLE I.—Descendants of **Alexander** (Stracathro), and **Thomas** and **John Don** (Dalbog).

Name. Period. Place.	Wives' Names. Date of Marriage.	Sons. Period.	Daughters. Period.	Daughters' Husbands. Date of Marriage.	Daughters' Children. Period.	Remarks.
(1) **I.—Alexander,** 1590– ? Stracathro.	?	Thomas, 1615–1672	?	?	?	(1) Our earliest recorded ancestor.
(1) **II.—Thomas,** 1615–1672 Stracathro, Dalbog.	Agnes Stewart, 1647 Born ? Died 1686.	John, 1650– ? James (2), 1652–1724	Agnes, 1648– ? Elizabeth (o), 1654– ? Margaret, 1660– ?	Alex. Greig, 1665 David Low, 1696	? ?	(1) See Edzell gravestone. (2) See Table II. (o) Extinct.
(1) **III.—John,** 1650–1710? Dalbog.	(1) ? (2) ?	Robert, 1686– ? Alexander, 1690– ? David, 1691– ? Thomas, 1697– ?	Jean, 1684– ? Jannet, 1688– ? Elspet, 1694– ? Ann (1), 1695– ? Ann (2), 1701– ?	Thomas Jollie, 1703 ? ? ? ? ?	?	(1) Said to have had 21 children, probably by two wives. 9 only registered. The sons founded Dons of Forfar and Dundee.

TABLE II.—Descendants of **James** (in Blackhall), son of Thomas and Agnes Stewart (Dalbog).

Name. Period. Place.	Wives' Names. Date of Marriage.	Sons. Period.	Daughters. Period.	Daughters' Husbands. Date of Marriage.	Daughters' Children. Period.	Remarks.
I.—**James,** 1652-1724 'Senior', in Blackhall. Table I.	(1) Isobel Fairweather, 1676? Born ? Died ?	Charles, 1678– James, 1682– ? Arthur, 1684– ?	Margaret, 1680– ?	John Gald, 1705.	?	See Memmuir Register.
	(2) Isobel Fyfe 1698 ? Born ? Died ?	(1) Alexander, 1700–1779 David, 1702– ?				(1) See Table III.
II.—**Charles,** 1678– ? Blackhall.	?	John, 1707 ?	?	?	?	
III.—**James,** 1682– ? 'Younger' in Blackhall.	?	(1) Alexander, 1717-1813 James, 1723– ?	Jannet, 1707– ? Isobel, 1715– ? Margaret, 1719– ? Catherine, 1721– ? Jean, 1728– ?	(2) William Reid.	?	(1) See Table IV. (2) A Burgess of Forfar.
IV.—**Arthur,** 1684– ? Muirside of Balzeordie.	?	John, 1723– ?	Anna, 1721– ? Margaret, ? 1725– ?	?	?	

TABLE III.—Descendants of **Alexander**, son of **James** and **Isobel Fyfe**.

Name. Period. Place.	Wives' Names. Date of Marriage.	Sons. Period.	Daughters. Period.	Daughters' Husbands. Date of Marriage.	Daughters' Children. Period.	Remarks.
1.—**Alexander,** 1700-1779 Blackhall, Ireland, Ballownie. Table II.	(1) Elizabeth Skair, 1724 Born Died 1730 ?	(1) Thomas, 1725-1809 James (2), 1728- ?	Isobel, 1726-	Ran away with an Army Officer, name unknown, 1741- ?	?	(1) Brechin Dons. (2) London Dons.
	(2) Janet Leighton, or Fairweather, 1731 Born Died 1741 ?	(1) David, 1733- ?	Janet, 1734-	Alex. Smith, 1747- ? 1757 (2) Pripollux	?	(1) Bonnyhard Dons. See Table VI. (2) Evidently 1757, compare Janet's age.
	(3) Janet Prophet, 1745 Born 1720 Died 1799	(1) Alexander, 1746-1808	Cathren, 1748-	Alex. Stowie, 1775 Millden	4 sons, 2 daughters, all extinct	(1) Ballownie Dons. See Table XI.
			Jean, 1751-	(1) Robert Goldie, 1773 (2) David Fettes, 1789	?	
			Christian, 1753	William Hood, 1788 Syde	3 sons and 3 daughters, all extinct	

TABLE IV.—Descendants of Alexander, son of James, Younger, in Blackhall.

Name. Period. Place.	Wives' Names. Date of Marriage.	Sons. Period.	Daughters. Period.	Daughters' Husbands. Date of Marriage.	Daughters' Children. Period.	Remarks.
I.—**Alexander,** 1717–1813? Ireland, Balzendie, Forfar. Table II.	Isobel Fairweather, 1760 Born ? Died ?	George (1), 1764–1814 William (2), 1766– ?	Jean, 1762– ? Margaret, 1768– ? Isobel, 1772– ? Janet, 1774– ? Anne, 1777– ?	?	?	(1) The Botanist. (2) Emigrated to America.
II.—**George,** 1764–1814. Edinburgh, Forfar.	Caroline Stuart, 1789 Born ? Died 1835?	George (o) (1), 1797–1856 David (o) (2), 1799–1840 Patrick Neill (3) 1806–76 James Edward Smith (o), 1807–61 Charles Lyell Linneas, 1810–57	Amelia Oliphant (o), 1794–1814			(1) Author of Don's *Millars Gardener's Dictionary.* (2) Professor of Botany, University College, London. (3) Author of Don's *Hortus Cantabridgensis*
III.—**Patrick, N.** 1806–76. Staffordshire, Kent.	Margaret Johnston, 1832 Born ? Died ?	George Alex., 1834– David (o), 1836– ?	Amelia Oliphant, 1838– Mary, 1842–			

TABLE IV. (*Continued*).—Descendants of **Alexander**, son of **James**, Younger, in Blackhall.

Name. Period. Place.	Wives' Names. Date of Marriage.	Sons. Period.	Daughters. Period.	Daughters' Husbands. Date of Marriage.	Daughters' Children. Period.	Remarks.
I.—**George, Alex.** 1834– Hawkhurst, Kent.	Louisa Prescott, 1866 Born	Malcolm Stuart, 1869–				
II.—**Malcolm, S.** 1869–	S. L. G. Vincent, 1894 Born		Louisa Margaret, 1895–			
IV.—**Charles, L.L.** 1810–57. Kent.	Anne Gorbutt, 1846 Born	Charles Stuart, 1850– Arthur Gorbutt, 1852–	Jane, 1854–			
I.—**Arthur, G.** 1852– Sevenoaks, Kent.	Adeline Fanny Brande, 1882 Born	George Arthur, 1883– Douglas Lyell, 1884– Edgar Brande, 1886– Geoffrey, 1890–	Elise Mary, 1888– Adeline Minnie, 1891–			

TABLE V.—Descendants of **Thomas**, son of **Alexander** and **Elizabeth Skair**.

Name. Period. Place.	Wives' Names. Date of Marriage.	Sons. Period.	Daughters. Period.	Daughters' Husbands. Date of Marriage.	Daughters' Children. Period.	Remarks.
I.—**Thomas**, 1725–1809. Dunninald. Brechin. Table III.	(1) Janet Leighton, 1760. Born Died 1765? (2) Janet McKenzie, 1768. Born ? Died ?	David (o) 1761–1834. Thomas, 1769–1855 James (1) 1773–1833 John, 1775– ? William, 1778–1851 Alexander, 1780–1794 Charles, 1782–1860 George, 1786–1814	Ann (o) 1763–1839			(1) See Table VII.
II.—**Thomas**, 1769–1855. Brechin.	Jean Barclay, 1797 Born 1773 Died 1841	David (o) 1802–1809	Jean, 1798–1872	Joseph Webster, 1820	Thomas David John George Jean Ann William Alexander	

TABLE V. (*continued*).—Descendants of **Thomas**, son of **Alexander** and **Elizabeth Skair**.

Name. Period. Place.	Wives' Names. Date of Marriage.	Sons. Period.	Daughters. Period.	Daughters' Husbands. Date of Marriage.	Daughters' Children. Period.	Remarks.
II.—**Thomas**, 1769-1855. (*Continued*.)	Jean Barclay (*Continued*)		Ann, 1800	Alex. Steven, Drowned 1843	Peter Ann Jean	
			Margaret, 1803–?	Unmarried.		
			Helen, 1805–1895	John V. Barton, 1830 Died 1872	William (1) Jean Helen Margaret Johanna (1) Johanna (2)	(1) Lives in Edinburgh.
			Mary, 1808 1886	David Troup, 1836 Died 1872	Jean Elizabeth David William Thomas Alexander Agnes	
			Agnes, 1811–1874	Robert Soppit, Died 1864	Thomas Elizabeth Jean	
			Elizabeth, 1813 1894	(1) Joseph Low	George John George Memes (1)	(1) Lives in Edinburgh.

TABLE V. (*continued*).—Descendants of **Thomas**, son of **Alexander** and **Elizabeth Skair**.

Name, Period, Place.	Wives' Names. Date of Marriage.	Sons. Period.	Daughters. Period.	Daughters' Husbands. Date of Marriage.	Daughters' Children. Period.	Remarks.
II.—**Thomas**, 1769–1855 (*Continued*).	Jean Barclay, (*Continued*).		Margaret, 1820–	(2) James Barclay	Jane Ann James William	
				Unmarried.		
III.—**John**, 1775–1837? Brechin.	Jean Macliar, ?		Anne	John Lawrence	Alexander (1)	(1) Doctor of Medicine in South Australia, married M. Kerr.
IV.—**William**, 1778–1851. Brechin.	Ann Duncan, ?	William (0) Thomas (0)	Mary (0)			Died young.
V.—**Charles**, 1782–1860. Sunderland.	(1) ? (2) Maria Hogg,	(1) Thomas (0)				(1) Died in infancy.

32

33

TABLE VI.—Descendants of **David**, son of **Alexander** and **Janet Leighton**.

Name. Period. Place.	Wives' Names. Date of Marriage.	Sons. Period.	Daughters. Period.	Daughters' Husbands. Date of Marriage.	Daughters' Children. Period.	Remarks.
I.—**David**, 1733–? Bonnyhard. Table III.	Jean Henderson, 1760. Born ? Died ?	Alexander, 1762–? David, 1770–1818.	Elizabeth, 1764–? Kathrine, 1766–?	Alexander Duncan, 1788. James Mackie, 1796. Westerton Balfour.	None Annie Jean James (1) Betsy Margaret John (2)	(1) Farner, Thorneyhill. (2) Doctor of Medicine, Brechin.
II.—**Alexander**, 1762–? Priestown, Dunlappie.	Agnes Smart, 1785. Born ? Died ?	David (o) 1787–1865. Alexander Duncan, 1793–1869.	Margaret, 1797–? Annie, 1772–? Isabella, 1790–? Jean, 1795–?	John Anderson, 1805. Robert Watson, 1807. William Coutts, John Smith, 1817. Dalfouper.	1 daughter None Ann Jean Elizabeth Kate Helen James	? ? ?
III.—**David**, 1770–1888. Bonnyhard.	Christian Hood, 1807. Born ? Died 1810.	David, 1809–1850.	Betty, 1797–	John Nicoll, Bogburn.		

TABLE VI. (continued).—Descendants of **David**, son of **Alexander** and **Janet Leighton**.

Name. Period. Place.	Wives' Names. Date of Marriage.	Sons. Period.	Daughters. Period.	Daughters' Husbands. Date of Marriage.	Daughters' Children. Period.	Remarks.
IV.—**David**, (o) 1787–1865. Canada.	Unmarried.					
V.—**Alexander Duncan,** 1793–1869. Brechin.	Elizabeth Cramond, 1821. Born 1792. Died 1867.		Isabella (o), 1722–22. Ann (o) 1824–81. Margaret (o), 1826–28. Janet or Jessie, 1829– Mary, . 1834–60. Jean, 1838–	Alex. Watson. (1) Andrew Simpson.	? Isabella, 1863. Elizabeth, 1865. Andrew, 1867. Alex. Don, 1869. Jane Ann, 1870. Jessie Helen, 1872. Margaret, 1874.	(1) Veterinary Surgeon; killed by fall from horse 1874, at Kendal, Westmoreland.
VI. **David,** 1809–50. Stonehaven.	?	?		?	?	

TABLE VII.—Descendants of **James**, son of **Thomas** and **Janet McKenzie**.

Name. Period. Place.	Wives' Names. Date of Marriage.	Sons. Period.	Daughters. Period.	Daughters' Husbands. Date of Marriage.	Daughters' Children. Period.	Remarks
1.—**James**, 1773–1833. Brechin. Table V.	Mary Carnegie, 1800. Born 1778. Died 1869.	James (1), 1801–74.	Anne, 1810–89.	Robert Don, (4) 1834.	Mary, 1835–	(1) See Table VIII.
		Thomas (2), 1804–78.	Mary (o), 1813–14.		Alexander, 1837–	(2) See Table IX.
		John (3), 1805.	Mary, 1816–		William (o), 1838–48.	(3) See Table X.
		William (o), 1807–20.				(4) See Table XI.

TABLE VIII.—Descendants of **James**, son of **James** and **Mary Carnegie**.

Name. Period. Place.	Wives' Names. Date of Marriage.	Sons. Period.	Daughters. Period.	Daughters' Husbands. Date of Marriage.	Daughter's Children. Period.	Remarks.
I.—**James**, 1801–74. Brechin. Table VII.	Jean Webster, 1833. Born 1803. Died 1887.	James, 1836– David, 1840– William, 1842–	Jean (o), 1834–46. Isobel (o), 1838–84. Mary Ann, 1846–	James Young, 1867.	George 1869 Jane Don 1872 John Loban 1874 Mary Ann 1876 James 1878 David Wm. 1880 Rachael 1881 Isobel Don 1882 Agnes Steel 1884 Elizabeth Mary Fairweather 1888	
II.—**James**, 1836– Brechin.	Isabella Brodie, 1888. Born 1849.	James (o), 1890–96.	Elizabeth Jane, 1889–			
III.—**David**, 1840– Natal.	Marie Nightingale, 1895. Born	David, 1896–				
IV.—**William**, 1842– India. Brechin.	Catherine Mary Hodgeton, 1896 Born					

TABLE IX.—Descendants of **Thomas**, son of **James** and **Mary Carnegie**.

Name. Period. Place.	Wives' Names. Date of Marriage.	Sons. Period.	Daughters. Period.	Daughters' Husbands. Date of Marriage.	Daughters' Children. Period.	Remarks.
I.—**Thomas**, 1803-78. Brechin. Balzeordie. Table VII.	Ann Low, 1836. Born 1818.	Andrew Low, 1842– Thomas, 1844– William Carnegie(o) 1853-77. Alexander, 1855–	Catherine, 1837–	William Swan, 1861. Died 1890. Moatmill, Balhungie.	Roger . . . 1862 Annie Low . . 1864 James Ogilvie . 1865 William Don . 1867 Agnes Maria . 1868 George Cunningham 1869 Hendrey Don . 1871 Andrew Don . 1874 Whitton Carnegie Don 1880	
			Margaret, 1840– Maria (o), 1849-72.	E. D. Nicol, 1863, Arbroath, Sunderland.	Alexander Andrew James Pinckney Quinton Harry Annie	
II.—**Andrew L.** 1842– London.	Annie Hendrey, 1869. Born 1847.	Thomas, 1870– Andrew Chalmers, 1877– William Hendrey, 1883– Arthur Durran, 1884–	Annie, 1873–			
III.—**Thomas**, 1844– London.	Annie Brown, 1879. Born 1847.	David, 1883– George Thomas, 1885–	Annie, 1881– Edith Jane, 1887– Mary Catherine, 1891–			
IV.—**Alexander**, 1855– New York.	Emma Lee.	Alexander Lee, 18 David, 18	Alice Gordon, 18 Annie Low, 18			

TABLE X.—Descendants of John, son of James and Mary Carnegie.

Name. Period. Place.	Wives' Names. Date of Marriage.	Sons. Period.	Daughters. Period.	Daughters' Husbands. Date of Marriage.	Daughters' Children. Period.	Remarks.
I.— **John,** 1805– Brechin. Table VII.	Jane Davidson, 1831 Born 1807. Died 1846.	John Davidson, 1834– James (o), 1838–49. Charles, 1843–76. David (o), 1844–48.	Mary Anne, 1832– Jane Anne, 1836–	James M. Ross, 1863. Montrose.	Margaret, 1865. John, 1867. Anna, 1871.	
II.— **John D.,** 1834– India. South Africa.	(1) Kate Baylie, 1863. Born Died 1875. (2) C. Brownlee, 18 Born	John Baylie, 1864– Alex. Brownlee, 18	Marion Lanfear, 1870– Kate Neville, 1871– Agnes, 18 Isabell Mary, 18 Jean Dorothy, 18	William Way, 1894.		
III.— **Charles,** 1843–76. China. Brechin.	Bessie Anderson, 1874. Born	Robert Anderson, 1875– Charles, 1876–				

TABLE XI.—Descendants of **Alexander** and **Jean Hood**.

Name. Period. Place.	Wives' Names. Date of Marriage.	Sons. Period.	Daughters. Period.	Daughters' Husbands. Date of Marriage.	Daughters' Children. Period.	Remarks.
I.—**Alexander**, 1746–1808. Ballownie. Table III.	Jean Hood, 1775. Born 1756. Died 1838.	John (o), 1781–1808. Alexander (1), 1782–1850. David, 1784–1863. Robert, 1788–1853. Thomas, 1790–1821. William, 1791–1850. (1) James (o), 1795–96. (2) James (o), 1798–1864.	Jean, 1777–1854. Jannet (o), 1778–1805. Mary (o), 1786–1861. Hannah (o), 1793–1804.	David Webster, 1798. Died 1850. Aged 84. Mill of Balrownie.	James, 1799. Alexander, 1801. David, 1803. Jean, 1805. Janet, 1807. Elizabeth, 1809. Mary, 1811. Ann, 1813. William, 1815. Isabella, 1819.	(1) See Table XII.
II.—**Alexander**, 1782–1850. Ballownie.	Jean Fullerton, 1820. Born 1792. Died 1871.	James (1), 1825–90. Alexander (2), 1827– Henry Speid (o), 1829–68. Robert (o), 1831–38. William Gerard (3), 1836–	Jean Valentine 1821–55. Margaret Fullerton 1833–	Walter Hood, 1850. Died 1862. Aged 62. Aberdeen. James Elder, 1849. Died 1868. Aged 56. Liverpool.	Jane, 1851–90. John, 1853– Jane, 1850–52. Janet Bruce, 1852–68. James, 1854–	(1) (2) (3) See Table XII.

TABLE XI. (*continued*).—Descendants of **Alexander** and **Jean Hood**.

Name. Period. Place.	Wives' Names. Date of Marriage.	Sons. Period.	Daughters. Period.	Daughters' Husbands. Date of Marriage.	Daughters' Children. Period.	Remarks.
(*Continued*). II.—**Alexander**, 1782–1850.	Jean Fullerton, 1820				(*Continued*). Helen Scott, 1855– Margaret, 1857– Mary Don, 1859– Christian Anderson, 1861–89.	
III.—**David**, 1784–1863. Keirsbeath. Fife.	Elizabeth Hogg, 1817. Born 1790. Died 1858.	David (o), 1818–55. Alexander (o), 1822–83. James (o), 1824–64.	Lillias (o), 1821–25. Jane Hood, 1827–	John F. Smith, 1847. Died 1849. Aged ? Edinburgh.	Eliza Bell, 1848– Joanna Jane, 1849–	
IV.—**Robert**, 1788–1853. Brechin.	Ann Don, 1834. Born 1810. Died 1889.	Alexander, 1837– William Carnegie (o) 1839–48.	Mary Carnegie, 1835–			
I.—**Alexander**, 1837– Edinburgh.	Joanna J. Smith, 1877. Born 1849.	Frederick Alex., 1878– Norman (o), 1885–6. Henry Wm., 1887	Ida Mary, 1889–			

TABLE XI. (*continued*).—Descendants of **Alexander** and **Jean Hood**.

Name. Period. Place.	Wives' Names. Date of Marriage.	Sons. Period.	Daughters. Period.	Daughters' Husbands. Date of Marriage.	Daughters' Children. Period.	Remarks.
V.—**William**, 1790–1850. Montreal, Canada.	Agnes McIntosh, 1827. Born Died 1876.	Robert, 1829– Alexander, 1831– William (o), 1833–35. James (o), 1834–75. David, 1836– William, 1838– Thomas (o), 1845–46.	Jane (o), 1828–32. Agnes Mary (o), 1840–44. Elizabeth Wright, 1843–78. Mary Jean (o), 1847–47.	James T. Dixon, 1874. Died 1896. Iowa.		

TABLE XI. (*continued*).—Descendants of **William** and **Agnes McIntosh** (America).

Name. Period. Place.	Wives' Names. Date of Marriage.	Sons. Period.	Daughters. Period.	Daughters' Husbands, Date of Marriage.	Daughters' Children. Period.	Remarks.
I.—**Robert,** 1829– Davenport Iowa, U.S.A.	Ottalie Dorothea Johanna Graack. Born 1859. 1886.	None.	None.			
II.—**James,** 1834–75. Rock Island, U.S.A.	Maggie McGhee, 1868. Born	William S. (o), 1869–95. Gussie (o), 1872–90.	Agnes (o), 1874–91.			
III.—**David,** 1836– Rock Island, U.S.A.	Agnes Jackson, 1874. Born	Louington (o), 1875–76. David (o), 1877–77. Elbert, 1885– De Forest, 1886.	Elizabeth, Gertrude, 1882– Irene Constance, 1888–			

TABLE XII. Descendants of Alexander and Jean Fullerton.

Name. Period. Place.	Wives' Names. Date of Marriage.	Sons. Period.	Daughters. Period.	Daughters' Husbands. Date of Marriage.	Daughters' Children. Period.	Remarks.
I.—**James,** 1825–90. Australia. Table XI.	(1) Zelia Laugá, 1857. Born 1830. Died 1876.	James, 1863– Henry Wm., 1865– Alexander, 1869–	Harriet Jane, 1858–75. Mary, 1861– Margaret, 1867–	Alex. McConan, 1881. Victoria, — Pringle. Sydney, —?	Six sons and daughters. ? ?	
	(2) Isabella Powstic, 1879. Born	Horace, 1881–	Gertrude, 1883–			
II.—**Alexander,** 1827– Fettercairn.	Jane Ann Ross, 1872. Born 1841.	Alexander, 1876– John (o), 1878–98. William, 1879–	Anne, 1872– Jeanie (o), 1874–75. Margaret, 1880– Christian (o), 1882–83. Alice (o), 1884–85.			
III.—**William, G.,** 1836– London.	(1) Louisa Jane Elliott, 1866. Born 1841. Died 1874.	Gilbert Elliott, 1867– Gerard Lewin (o), 1870–80. William Walton, 1872–	Caroline Moore, 1868– Mabel Mylius, 1869–	Matthew Robin, 1895. Glasgow.	Robert Douglas, 1896.	
	(2) Jean Ann Fairweather, 1889. Born 1852.	David Fairweather, 1893–				

II.—TABLE OF NAMES.

RELATIVE FREQUENCY OF CHRISTIAN NAMES OF DONS RECORDED IN FOREGOING.

Males.	No.	Males.	No.	Females.	No.	Females.	No.
David	19	Frederick	1	Jean, Jane	15	Louisa	1
Alexander	18	Norman	1	Ann, Annie Anna	14	Helen	1
James	16	Gilbert	1	Margaret	13	Betty	1
William	15	Gerard	1	Mary	11	Marion	1
Thomas	11	Gussie	1	Isobel	7	Kate	1
John	8	Louington	1	Janet	6	Harriet	1
Charles	6	Elbert	1	Elizabeth	6	Gertude	1
George	6	De Forest	1	Agnes	5	Caroline	1
Robert	5			Catherine	4	Mabel	1
Arthur	3			Christian	2	Maria	1
Henry	3			Amelia	2	Edith	1
Andrew	2			Mary Ann	2	Hannah	1
Patrick	1			Alice	2	Lillias	1
Malcolm	1			Elspet	1	Ida	1
Douglas	1			Jane Ann	1	Irene	1
Edgar	1			Elise	1		
Geoffrey	1			Adeline	1		
Total	25		125				108

III.—TABLE OF OCCUPATIONS.

ABSTRACT SHOWING THE OCCUPATIONS OF THE GROWN UP MEN RECORDED IN THE TABLES.

I.—**Lairds, Farmers and Gardeners** . 40

II.—**Trades and Handicrafts** . . 23

III.—**Merchants and Manufacturers** . 22

IV.—**Bankers** 7

V.—**Professional,** including Lawyers, Doctors, Ministers, **Engineers** 19

VI.—**Unclassified and Unknown** 35

Total . 146

Chapter V.

THE EARLIER DONS.

Y FATHER'S statement that the Dons settled in Angus, from Aberdeen, only about the period of the Reformation in the Sixteenth century, must, in the light of records with which he was unacquainted, now be received with reservation; because, although not absolutely disproved by those records, it is rendered exceedingly improbable.

The Aberdeen origin moreover, is unlikely; because, that county never was, like East Perth, a primary centre of the name; and, further, we have positive proof that the Dons were already numerous in the Brechin district early in the seventeenth century, and did not then appear as if recent arrivals.

The weight of evidence, therefore, is, that the Family has existed in north Angus from an indefinite period.

The first recorded name in the locality is in Deuchar's Extracts, year 1608: the person, Alexander Don, Chapman, Fettercarden. He was evidently a man of some substance or his will would not have been proved, in Edinburgh; but that he was a direct ancestor there is nothing to show; although every probability that he was a relative, belonging to the original stock.

NOTE.—A Chapman of that period was merely a travelling merchant, carrying his wares (mostly clothing) either on his own back, or on a pack-horse; the term is a form of the Anglo-Saxon, *ceap-man*, cheapman; hence, 'Cheapside'—place of bargains. His status was superior to that of a pedlar, or peddler, who hawked small wares in a basket: (Old English *ped*—a basket).

The next recorded name is also an Alexander; whose existence in Stracathro is incidentally mentioned, as 'Cautioner' for his son Thomas at the marriage 1647, (Edzell Register). My father knew nothing of him; much less that he lived in Stracathro, and, may, for aught known have been farmer in that very Ballownie, which was occupied by his descendants two centuries after his time! It is possible the Fettercairn Chapman may have been the father of this Alexander; but it is, perhaps, more likely the latter was nearly connected with the contemporary Brechin Dons of untraced pedigree.

Among those Brechin Dons were two named James; contemporaries, and probably cousins; and who appear to have married sisters, of the name Cramond. (Brechin Baptismal Register.) One of them is described as farmer of Airdo, in Stracathro: and, at the date—1655—being a contemporary of Thomas of Dalbog, may have been his own brother, and thus son of the Stracathro Alexander. A little later —1672—the same Register, discloses another Alexander, husband to Isobel Erskyn; and also an Arthure—1684—husband to Katharen Deass; both of whom were probably sons of one of the James's mentioned in the previous generation.

I can merely speculate, however, on the probable relationship of these untraced Brechin Dons of two and a half centuries ago; my genealogy really begins with Alexander, father of Thomas.

I. The Dalbog DONS.

(1) **Alexander** (of Stracathro) 1590 to —?

This man is the bedrock upon which we must build our Family Pedigree.

As before said, we only know of him incidentally. Considering that, the Edzell Register of the seventeenth century is very imperfect and fragmentary, it is, indeed, more than fortunate that the marriage of Thomas Don and Agnes Stewart, in 1647, is so clearly and fully recorded, and even includes mention of the paternal father. For, from that date and union, we can trace direct, lineal, unbroken descent.

(2) **Thomas** 1651 (?) to 1672.

The date of his birth is conjectural, but we know that of his marriage and death. We know nothing of his wife, **Agnes Stewart** further than, that she belonged to Edzell; and, as the West Water flowed between them, he must have forded the river to do his courting; for there was no Inchbare bridge in those days!

My father states Thomas was joint tenant in Dalbog, (partly an arable, partly a sheep farm) with a brother named John ; but, as we have no trace of the existence of this John, I think there must have been some confusion on the part of my father's informant over Thomas's supposed brother, and his own son John, who succeeded him in the tenancy.

As the Edzell Register of Baptisms only begins in 1684, we have no record of Thomas's children except incidentally. He must have had at least the following, with approximate date of births :

(1) **Agnes,** 1648 to —

(2) **John,** 1650 to —

(3) **James,** 1652 to —

(4) **Elizabeth,** 1654 to —

(5) **Margaret,** 1660 to —

(1) **Agnes** 1648 to — ?

Appears to have married very young—1665—**Alexander Grieg,** of Aberlemno (Table I. Edzell Marriages 2).

(4) **Elizabeth,** 1654 to 1661.

Died, as recorded on the tombstone, 1661.

(5) **Margaret,** 1660 — ?

Married **David Low,** in 1696 (Edzell Marriages 4).

It is from the tombstone in Edzell Churchyard that we learn of the death of Thomas and his wife. My father spoke of that precious relic as broken and defaced, but evidently from hearsay, as it fortunately is neither. In July 1895, myself and cousin James Don, solicitor, Brechin, found the stone, set against a wall, a few feet from the old Dalbog burying ground ; it is a fine Carmyllie pavement slab, 6½ by 4 feet ; the best old stone in the churchyard ; in excellent preservation, artistically carved, and inscribed round the circumference as follows :

'Here lys Thomas Don who died in the year 1672, and Agnes 'Stewart, his spouse, who died in the year 1686, and Elizabeth Don, 'ther daughter, who died in the year of God 1661.'

There are three panels on the stone ; the upper one adorned with figures of cherubs, and with some poetry, of which the first line can be deciphered ; beginning :

> 'Sweet Jesus who shall give me wings.'

The second panel holds a monogram of the letters T.A.D., and, on each side the initials of the recorded dead, T.D. A.S. and E.D. ; the third panel is blank.

This stone was, of course, erected after 1686 ; probably by the son John, who may have intended the empty panel for his own record : and which would have been filled had his family displayed similar filial devotion as he did himself. At his death, Thomas could hardly have been over sixty ; the only other thing we know about him is that, in 1666 (time of the Plague, and year of the great Fire in London), he was made an Elder of the Kirk at Edzell.

(3) **John**, 1650 to 1710 ?

We have no record of his birth, marriage or death ; but my father states he was reputed to have had twenty-one children ; and probably, therefore, had two wives. He succeeded his father in the farm, being the eldest son, and probably married about 1673. Nine children are recorded to him after the opening of the Edzell Baptismal Register in 1684, as follows (Table I., Edzell Baptisms, 1 to 9) :—

    (1) **Jean** 1684 to
    (2) **Robert** 1686 to
    (3) **Jannett** 1688 to
    (4) **Alexander** 1690 to
    (5) **David** 1691 to
    (6) **Elspet** 1694 to
    (7) **Ann** (1) 1695 to
    (8) **Thomas** 1697 to
    (9) **Ann** (2) 1701 to

(1) **Jean**, 1684 to —

Married **Thomas Jollie** in 1703 (Edzell Marriages 5).

I know nothing of the history of the other members of John's large family, beyond that some of his sons migrated to Forfar and Dundee, and so founded the Dons of these Burghs :

II. The Forfar and Dundee DONS.

The Dons of these towns have long been linen manufacturers, and opulent leading citizens. But they have long ceased to have any intimacy with their original relations in the Brechin district; and, beyond their descent from John of Dalbog, I am ignorant of their subsequent genealogy.

I now come to describe;

III. The Blackhall DONS.

I am here at once confronted with a difficulty. My father regarded James (senior) in Blackhall, as son of John, and grandson of Thomas in Dalbog. But a study and comparison of the Edzell and Menmuir Registers—to which my father had no access, renders this succession impossible; for, John of Dalbog and James of Blackhall were absolute contemporaries, and had sons and daughters of similar ages. I have closely thought out the matter, and come to the conclusion that, as there was confusion in my father's account between Thomas's supposed brother John, and own son John, so there was also a mistake in the relationship of James. He apparently was not the grandson, but son of Thomas, and therefore a younger brother of John. On this almost certain assumption I proceed.

(4) **James**, 1652 to 1724 (Table II.).

He must be described as senior in Blackhall for a reason afterwards apparent. As there is no record of his birth, so there is no date of his going to Blackhall, or of his marriage or marriages. I place both these latter events shortly after his father's death in 1672— say about 1676. The next question is, who were his wife, or wives? My father says, Isabel Fyfe; whom he names as his own great grandmother; but Alexander Fairweather, the accurate historian of his own family, says Isobel Fairweather; daughter, or granddaughter, of John Fairvedder, who was in Blackhall in the previous generation; and sister to Alexander Fairweather in Little Cruick, and George Fairweather in Mill of Balhall; all of which seems to be borne out by the inscription on the Menmuir tombstone. I think it very unlikely my father did not know the name of his great grandmother, but at the same time there is the strongest evidence in favour of the Fairweather theory. The explanation seems to be that both historians are right; and, if this be assumed, discrepancies and confusion disappear.

James, therefore, apparently married, first, **Isobel Fairweather**, in whom was vested the life rent of Blackhall, a succession which at that time often descended in the female line (Cruickshank). She died probably about 1690, and the farm was then taken on a nineteen years' lease; and continued on a second nineteen, which lapsed in 1728, as indicated in my father's memoir.

The recorded children of James and Isobel Fairweather are as follows (Table II., Menmuir Baptisms):—

    (1) **Charles** 1678 to —
    (2) **Margaret** 1680 to —
    (3) **James** 1682 to —
    (4) **Arthur** 1684 to —

(1) **Charles,** 1678 to —
Married—wife unknown; had a son baptized **John** in 1707, (Menmuir Baptisms, 1).

(2) **Margaret,** 1680 to —
Married **John Gald,** 1705 (Menmuir Marriages 1).

(3) **James,** 1682 to —
Always registered 'Younger in Blackhall' up to his father's death in 1724. Married, wife unknown, and had the following recorded children (Menmuir Baptisms, 2, 3, 4, 5, 6, 9, 14).

    (1) **Jannet** 1707 to —
    (2) **Isobel** 1715 to —
    (3) **Alexander** 1717 to 1813?
    (4) **Margaret** 1719 to —
    (5) **Catherine** 1721 to —
    (6) **James** 1723 to —
    (7) **Jean** 1728 to —

(1) **Jannet,** 1707 to —
Supposed to have married **William Reid,** a Burgess of Forfar (G. A. Don).

(3) **Alexander,** 1717 to 1813.
Father of the 'Botanist,' of whom hereafter.
I have no account of the other members of James the
'Younger's' family.

(4) **Arthur,** 1684 to — (Table II.).
Was a small farmer at Muirside of Balzeordie. Married—wife unknown—and had children (Menmuir Baptisms, 7, 8, 11) :—
    (1) **Anna** 1721 to —
    (2) **John** 1723 to —
    (3) **Margaret** 1725 to —
The history of this family is unrecorded.

NOTE.—Of James (senior's) sons, Charles and James 'Younger,' are described as of Blackhall; from which they either worked for their father, or held some position in the tenancy. My impression is, that, while their father was tenant of the farm, they were sub-tenants in the Mill; in fact 'Millers.' I have alluded to this before, and will afterwards show it has bearing on the inscription on the Menmuir monument.

James, senior, apparently married **Isobel Fyfe** about 1698, and had two sons.

(1) **Alexander,** 1700 to 1779 (Tables II. and III.), of whom hereafter; and,

(2) **David,** 1702 to — who died young.

NOTE.—James, senior, died in 1724, towards the end of the second nineteen years' lease of Blackhall; and was succeeded by his son Alexander, who farmed on his mother's behalf, till his removal to Ireland about 1728. The only other facts known about James are that, in 1706, he was an Elder in the Kirk as his father Thomas had been before him; and that he is supposed to have shared in the erection of the Menmuir Monument. His three elder sons, Charles, James and Arthur, as well as his widow Isobel Fyfe, are no more mentioned after 1728.

The following is an account of the Menmuir Monument, now built into the south wall of the church.

It bears the inscription :—

'1717. This Monument was erected at the charge and expense
'of Alexander Fairweather in Little Cruick, George Fairweather,

'in Mill of Balhall, and James Don, at the Mill of Blackhall, and
'Alexander Smith in Teagertown, in Memory of their Ancestors
'Residenters in this paroch, and for themselves, Wives and Children
'and their posterity.'

Of this inscription, Alexander Fairweather, historian, writing in 1875, says :—' There is the very strongest probability that the two 'brothers mentioned on the monument, and their two sisters, who 'were married to James Don and Alexander Smith, were the sons 'and daughters of John Fairvedder, who was in Blackhall in the 'previous generation.'

Of course the assumption here is that it is James Don ' senior' who is mentioned on the monument ; for I doubt if my father or Alexander Fairweather knew of the existence of a James ' younger.' But I infer it was the latter who is really meant, from the expression '*at* the *Mill* of Blackhall'; for, had it been the 'senior,' he would have been described as *in* Blackhall like other tenants. This strengthens the belief that the 'senior' was sole tenant of the farm, and explains the anomaly of the junior son Alexander succeeding to the tenancy; because the 'younger' James was, and remained simply the 'Miller.' Of course, he could, his mother being a Fairweather, also legitimately speak as on the monument of his 'ancestors in the paroch.'

The monument in question was originally set up at the burying ground of the Fairweathers ; but in course of time became detached. When the Church was repaired in 1837, by contract with my uncle Robert, the builder, he found the slab derelict in the churchyard ; and, prompted by the filial instincts of his race, rescued it, and built it—perhaps with indifferent legal warranty—into the south wall of the Church, where it now is.

Many years afterwards its prominent position in the wall offended the taste of a new Minister, who, in his æsthetic zeal, sought to remove it ; which gratuitous proposition, on the part of a stranger, so roused Alexander, the historian, and David Fairweather, Laughaugh, that they threatened an interdict ; the agent of the principal heritor, also cautioned the minister not to meddle with it ; and he quietly dropped the idea. So it remains ; a fixture now by the proscription of time ; so may it continue ; secure alike against the ravages of years, and all envious iconoclastic zeal !

CHAPTER VI.

THE 'BOTANIST' DONS.

N THIS Chapter we arrive at a period in the Family History, from which the Pedigree descends with certainty. Here and there a date may still be doubtful, but can always be given with close approximation. I shall here trace a very interesting family branch, under the apposite and well-warranted term, ' Botanist Dons '; descended from Alexander, son of James 'younger,' of Blackhall; which, although junior to the branch of Alexander son of James 'senior,' may yet be conveniently considered first. For much, and the whole of the latter part of the account here given, I am indebted to a kindred genealogical enthusiast, George Alexander Don, of Hawkhurst, Kent. This section might also be fairly called the English branch of the Family.

Alexander, 1717 to 1813? (Tables II. and IV., Menmuir Baptisms 4.)

The inferred date of his death may be under but not overstated; for, he was almost a centenarian; known from the fact that his grandson Patrick, born in 1806, could remember him, as others also described him—a very, very old man, living in Forfar. About 1760, and when over forty, he married his cousin, removed, **Isobel Fairweather,** daughter of George Fairweather in Milltown of Balhall (see Menmuir Monument), by whom he had the following children (Menmuir Baptisms 16 to 22) :—

    (1) **Jean,** 1762 to —
    (2) **George,** 1764 to 1814.
    (3) **William,** 1766 to —
    (4) **Margaret,** 1768 to —
    (5) **Isobel,** 1772 to —
    (6) **Jannet,** 1774 to —
    (7) **Anna,** 1777 to —

NOTE.—Of these daughters I have no further record; and of William nothing beyond that he was a watchmaker, and emigrated to America. Of George, being the famous 'Botanist,' we have full account. The old man, their father, was a small farmer; first in Ireland, where he apparently succeeded, or was left in charge, by his uncle Alexander, when the latter removed to Ballownie in 1742; afterwards on the small holdings of Muirside of Balzeordie, and Meadowburn; and finally spent his declining years with his son George, in Forfar, where he died and was buried. Like many crofters of his time he combined the trade of shoemaking with farming, at which he would work when outdoor labour was suspended or slack; even in his very old age he loved to potter in Forfar at that trade. St. Crispin's alliance with small farming, was a curious but common one in old Scotland; and even existed within my own recollection.

(2) **George, 1764 to 1814** (Table IV.).

Was, and is, widely known as the 'Forfar Botanist'; and stands out the most famous Don in this history. In 1789, he married **Caroline Stuart**, related to the Oliphants of Gask; this curiously, was the second intermarriage between the Dons and Oliphants; the first being recorded in Deuchar's Extracts, year 1618. By her, who died in 1835, he had the following children :—

(1) **Amelia Oliphant**, 1794 to 1814.
(2) **George**, 1797 to 1856.
(3) **David**, 1799 to 1840.
(4) **Patrick Neill**, 1806 to 1876.
(5) **James Edward Smith**, 1807 to 1861.
(6) **Charles Lyell Linneus**, 1810 to 1857.

NOTE.—The whole Family of Don may well be proud of George the Botanist; a man who, by sheer native intelligence and force of character, achieved a lasting position among Scottish Botanists. Born on 11th Oct. 1764, at the remote farm of Ireland, he could only have had a scanty education; but some innate love of plants probably led to his being bred a gardener; in his boyhood he had scoured the hill sides in many an excursion, and this early training fitted him for his after career. He soon became a horticulturist of such note as to be appointed Curator of the Botanic Gardens, Edinburgh; a position which he resigned, on renting, or owning, the house and grounds of 'Dove Hillock,' as a nurseryman, close to the town of Forfar. In this position, he became not only a botanical discoverer, but a thoroughly practical forester, and as such afforested several of the large estates in the neighbourhood. His reputation as a botanist is based on the discovery of certain Alpine plants, hitherto unknown in Scotland, on the higher summits of the Grampians, especially in the Clova district. These he found, all alone by extraordinary excursions and effort such as only a man of exceptionally powerful physique could have borne. In pursuit of his beloved science he often walked thirty and forty miles a-day ; cooking his meals on the hillside, and sleeping in the open ; which exposure, however, probably hastened his end, for he died, comparatively young, at fifty.

It is said he often became so absorbed in his wide and prolonged rambles as to forget the days of the week ; which lapses on one occasion caused him to be detected, in the Braemar district, actually breaking the Sabbath in pursuit of Botany ! His fame and published discoveries brought him the acquaintance of such scientific savants as, Dr. Patrick Neill, Edinburgh ; Sir Joseph Banks ; Sir James Edward Smith ; and Sir Charles Lyell, Bart., of Kinnordy ; names afterwards refected in those of his sons.

Many curious anecdotes are recorded of this remarkable man, some of which are related in a memoir by Knox, in the 'Scottish Naturalist' 1881.—Bishop Goodenough, of Carlisle, made a pilgrimage to Forfar to see the Botanist ; and on asking a native where he could find George Don, was promptly referred to a Colonel George Don (probably afterwards General Sir George Don, K.C.B.) who chanced to be passing up the street : the Bishop, noting the military bearing of the colonel, said : ' No, that cannot be the man I want ' ; upon which the native said, ' You'll want Doo Hillock,' and at once conducted him to the nursery, where he found the botanist hard at work.

Altogether, we must view George as a most exceptional man, both physically and mentally ; one literally head and shoulders above his contemporaries.

It is perhaps even more exceptional that his genius for Botany largely descended to his sons, who were all bred nurserymen.

(1) **Amelia Oliphant**, 1794 to 1814.
Died, at Forfar, unmarried.

(2) **George**, 1797 to 1856.

Born at Forfar; died, unmarried.

NOTE.—This George, went to London as a fully-equipped botanist; and became Fellow of the Linnean Society, and author of several botanical works; including 'Don's Millar's Gardeners' Dictionary,' (of which I have a copy in 4 vols.); a stupendous work, begun in 1831, ended in 1838, but never finished, through default of the Publishers; also of 'Loudon's Encyclopedia of Plants,' etc.

(3) **David**, 1799 to 1840.

Born in Forfar, died in London; married; no issue.

NOTE.—Another very able botanist, who, when a youth, accompanied his father to Edinburgh; where his decided botanical genius attracted the attention of Dr. Patrick Neill, and others; through whom he entered the employment of Messrs. Dickson, the eminent nurserymen near Edinburgh. In 1819, he went to London, under the auspices of a Mr. Lambert, who then possessed the finest collection of rare plants in the metropolis. In 1822, he became Librarian of the Linnean Society, in which position he wrote many valuable monographs, on various departments of systematic botany; and also, edited an account of his father's Scottish Alpine discoveries. In 1836, he was appointed to the Chair of Botany, King's College, London; but had little opportunity of distinguishing himself in that position, as he was attacked by a malignant tumour of the lip (epithelioma), which caused his death in December 1840.

(4) **Patrick Neill**, 1806 to 1876.

Born in Edinburgh; died in Kent.

Married, in 1832, Margaret Johnston (partly of French extraction) and had children:

       (1) **George Alexander**, 1834 to —
       (2) **David**, 1836 to —; died in infancy.
       (3) **Amelia Oliphant**, 1838 to —
       (4) **Mary**, 1842 to —

(1) **George Alexander**, 1834 to —

Born in Staffordshire; educated in London; bred a gardener at Dalmeny Park, Edinburgh; a valued contributor to these Memoirs.

He held appointments in Scotland; and also as head gardener to Lord Gough, County Galway, Ireland, and the Right Hon. G. J. Goschen, in Sussex; finally succeeded his father at Bedgebury Park, Kent; now residing at Hawkhurst, Kent.

In 1866, he married **Louisa Prescott**, and had issue:

(1) **Malcolm Stuart**, 1869 to —

Who married in 1894, **Sarah Louisa Gertrude Vincent**, by whom he has a daughter:

(1) **Louisa Margaret**, 1895 to —

(3) **Amelia Oliphant**, 1838 to —

Born in Staffordshire; living in Sevenoaks; unmarried.

(4) **Mary**, 1842 to —

Born in Surrey; living at Marden, Kent; unmarried.

NOTE.—Patrick Neill, following his brothers to London, and, being a capable botanist, soon held good appointments; the last with the Right Hon. A. Beresford Hope, Bedgebury Park, Kent. He was author of 'Don's Hortus Cantabridgensis'; and was likewise an authority on Entomology.

(5) **James Edward Smith**, 1807 to 1861.

Born in Forfar; died in Kent, unmarried.

Also went to England as a young gardener, and secured good appointments; the last being at Earl Amherst's, Knowle, Kent.

(6) **Charles Lyell Linneas**, 1810 to 1857.

Born in Forfar; killed in attempting to stop a runaway horse, in 1857, at Bedgebury Park, Kent.

He married, 1846, **Anne Gorbutt**, and had children:

(1) **Charles Stuart**, 1850 to —
(2) **Arthur Gorbutt**, 1852 to —
(3) **Jane**, 1854 to —

(1) **Charles Stuart**, 1850 to —

Born in Kent: educated at Queen Elizabeth's Grammar School, Sevenoaks, and Cambridge University; in the Civil Service; living in London; unmarried.

(2) **Arthur Gorbutt**, 1852 to —

Born in Kent: educated at Queen Elizabeth's School, Sevenoaks; studied medicine at University College, London; M.R.C.S. Eng. 1875; L.R.C.P. Lond. 1876. Practices in Sevenoaks. Married, 1882, **Adeline Fanny Brande**, daughter of the Rev. W. T. C. Brande, Rector of Barton-cum-Coates, and has children:

    (1) **George Arthur**, 1883 to —
    (2) **Douglas Lyell**, 1884 to —
    (3) **Edgar Brande**, 1886 to —
    (4) **Elise Mary**, 1888 to —
    (5) **Geoffrey**, 1890 to —
    (6) **Adeline Minnie**, 1891 to —

(3) **Jane**, 1854 to —

Born in Kent; living, unmarried, with her mother in London.

NOTE.—Charles Lyell Linneus was, like his brothers, a capable botanist and horticulturist. He held several good appointments, the last at Bedgebury Park, where he met his death.

Here ends the 'Botanist Dons.'

Chapter VII.

THE BRECHIN DONS.

IN THIS chapter I revert to Alexander, son of James (senior) in Blackhall, by his (second) wife Isobel Fyfe.

I. **Alexander**, 1700 to 1779 (Tables II. and III.) Was born at Blackhall, and through three wives, (respectively), became the leading ancestor of the three chief branches of the Dons of Angus; namely :—

(1) The Brechin Dons.
(2) The Bonnyhard Dons.
(3) The Ballownie Dons.

By his first wife, he had two sons and one daughter.
By his second wife, one son and one daughter.
By his third wife, one son and three daughters.
I will consider these families in three distinct chapters.

Alexander, on the death of his father in 1724, and when about twenty-three years of age, succeeded to the tenancy of Blackhall; which he farmed, apparently on behalf of his mother, until the expiry of the lease in 1728. In the same year he removed to the hill farm of Ireland; and from thence, in 1742, to Ballownie. His children were born, as I will relate, on all of these three farms.

In 1724, while at Blackhall, he married his first wife, **Elizabeth Skair**, daughter of David Skair, of Balconnel and Burnside, Menmuir (A. Fairweather); through her he became the ancestor of the

BRECHIN DONS,

by the following children :—

I. **Thomas**, 1725 to 1809.
II. **Isobel**, 1726 to —
III. **James**, 1728 to —

whom I will describe in inverse order.

(3) **James,** 1728 to —

Born in Ireland (Menmuir Baptisms 13).

NOTE.—When a young man, he went to London; where he prospered in business, and left descendants, of whom, however, I have no record.

(2) **Isobel,** 1726 to —

Born in Blackhall (Menmuir Baptisms 12). Her brief career is far too romantic to let die; I give it, chiefly from my father's account, but also with incidents mentioned to me by my mother; in whose younger days, the gossips of the neighbourhood used to relate tales of Isobel, seventy years after the wayward girl had disappeared from history.

Isobel, when a mere girl of fifteen or sixteen, was noted in the countryside for great beauty, agility and daring; among other feats, she rode her father's horses, standing bare-backed in circus fashion. Her dash and good looks naturally brought admirers; including an officer of a marching regiment, which then had a detachment in Brechin. An elopement with this man being feared, her father kept strict watch and ward over her. But the order to march came, and the love-stricken officer resolved to carry her off with him at all hazards. So, he set out, on a moonlight night, for lonely Ireland, with a half dozen of his trusty men, to abduct the farmer's daughter. On arrival there, he demanded her; but was of course met with a direct refusal, and the door bolted in his face; Isobel, however, it is said, escaped by a window, into the arms of her lover, and was borne off. Her indignant father, next day hurried to Brechin, to invoke the arm of the law; which legal limb, however, declared itself powerless to effect a rescue from the midst of an armed force; so she was reluctantly let go. She married her abductor (name unrecorded) and followed him to the campaign in the 'Low Countrie' of Germany. On the eve of a battle (probably Dettingen 1743) her husband, with a presentiment of evil, gave her in charge to the Surgeon of the Regiment; on the morrow, she was a very young widow. The medical officer afterwards married her; and she marched with him during the rest of the campaign, ultimately dying from hardship and exposure.

So ended the brief and tragic career of a fascinating, and high-spirited if wayward girl. It has been suggested, with some plausibility, that her moonlight elopement was truly an escape from cruel drudgery, imposed by an unsympathetic stepmother; so that, proud Isobel, may, after all, have been as much sinned against as sinning.

(1) **Thomas**, 1725 to 1809. (Tables III. and V.; Menmuir Baptisms 10).

Born in Blackhall; died in Brechin, and was apparently buried in Menmuir; twice married; founder of the existing Brechin Dons.

NOTE.—He did not follow farming like his forbears; but carried on the business of a carpenter and millwright at Duninald, near Montrose, and in Brechin. I have heard him described as a strong-built, fair complexioned man; known in his district for unswerving integrity in all relations of life. His death is inscribed on the Menmuir tombstone.

His first wife, was his cousin **Janet Leighton**, daughter of David Leighton, farmer, Balrownie; by his wife Ann Skair, a sister of his mother (A. Fairweather); by her he had two children:

I. **David** 1761 to 1834. (Table V.).

Merchant and Baillie in Brechin; where he acquired considerable wealth: died unmarried.

II. **Ann** 1763 to 1839.

Died in Brechin; unmarried.

Thomas' second wife was **Janet McKenzie**, whom he married in 1768, (Brechin Marriages 5); and by whom he had the golden number of seven sons.

(1) **Thomas** 1769 to 1855.
(2) **James** 1773 to 1833.
(3) **John** 1775 to 1837?
(4) **William** 1778 to 1851.
(5) **Alexander** 1780 to 1794.
(6) **Charles** 1782 to 1860.
(7) **George** 1786 to 1814.

These sons were mostly bred to trades in Brechin; the name, however, entirely descended through James, whom, therefore, I shall take last.

I. **Thomas** 1769 to 1855. (Tables III and V.)

NOTE.—Succeeded to his father's business; died at an advanced age—a worthy and respected citizen of Brechin. He married in 1797, **Jean Barclay**, of Montrose, (Brechin Marriages 10), and by her redressed the balance of his father's seven sons, in eight daughters, and one son; namely:

(1) **David** 1802 to 1809. Died in infancy.

(2) **Jean** 1798 to 1872. (Table V.)

NOTE.—Married **Joseph Webster**, and had six sons and two daughters. I well remember her; like her sisters, who were the handsomest women in Brechin, she was a fine, stately woman. One of her sons rose to high civic dignity in Melbourne, Australia.

(3) **Ann.** 1800 to —

Married, **Alexander Steven**, and had one son and two daughters.

NOTE.—A. Steven, a mariner, sailed with Captain Cargill of Arbroath, and was lost with him and his son Peter Cargill, off that port, in a memorable storm (which I can remember) November, 1843.

(4) **Margaret.** 1803 to —

Died unmarried.

(5) **Helen.** 1805 to 1895.

Married in 1830, **John V. Barton**, who died in 1872, and had one son and five daughters.

(6) **Mary.** 1808 to 1886.

Married in 1836, **David Troup**, who died in 1872, and had four sons and three daughters.

(7) **Agnes.** 1811 to 1874.

Married **Robert Soppit**, who died in 1864; and had one son and two daughters.

(8) **Elizabeth.** 1813 to 1894.

Married (1) **Joseph Low**, by whom she had three sons; and (2) **James Barclay**, by whom she had two sons and one daughter.

(9) **Margaret.** 1820 to —

Unmarried.

(3) **John.** 1775 to 1837. (Table V.)

A mason builder in Brechin; married **Jean Machar**, and had a daughter,

(1) **Anne.** ?

Married **John Lawrence** of Greenden.

(4) **William.** 1778 to 1851. (Table V.)

Was a skilful maker of tools, and mechanical instruments in Brechin; a fair, spare, delicate man as I can remember him. Married **Ann Duncan**, and had two sons and one daughter, all of whom died young and unmarried.

 (1) **William.**
 (2) **Thomas.**
 (3) **Mary.**

(5) **Alexander.** 1780 to 1794. (Table V.)

Died young: my father records, ' he was remarkable for the beauty of his person.'

(6) **Charles.** 1782 to 1860. (Table V. Stracathro Baptisms 8.)

Became a wine merchant in Sunderland. Twice married (1) to one whose name I do not have; (2) to **Maria Hogg**, by whom he had a son.

 (1) **Thomas.** ? who died in infancy.

(7) **George.** 1786 to 1814. (Table V. Stracathro Baptisms 10). Died unmarried.

I now revert to James, through whom the name descended.

(2) **James.** 1793 to 1833. (Table VII. Brechin Marriages 11.) Married **Mary Carnegie**, and had the following children.

 (1) **James.** 1801 to 1874.
 (2) **Thomas.** 1803 to 1878.
 (3) **John.** 1805 to —
 (4) **William.** 1807 to 1820.
 (5) **Anne.** 1810 to 1889.
 (6) **Mary.** (1) 1813 to 1814.
 (7) **Mary.** (2) 1816 to —

NOTE.—James had a forge in Brechin, through which he acquired considerable property: he died, aged 59, a much respected citizen. His wife, Mary Carnegie, died at the age of 91, on 21st Feby., 1869. She came of a grand Angus stock, and two of her brothers served under Nelson in the great French War. She was the most typical specimen of the old lady of a bygone age I can remember: comely, kindly, couthie; an ideal grandmother. Her dress; bodiless gown; tippet; close fitting cap, fastened with a broad black ribbon and top knot, was exactly that in the well known portrait of the good Hannah More.

(1) **James.** 1801 to 1874. (Table VIII.)

Married, 1833, his relative, **Jean Webster**, (Table XI.) daughter of David Webster, farmer, Mill of Balrownie, and had;

    (1) **Jean.** 1834 to 1846 —died a girl.
    (2) **James.** 1836 to —
    (3) **Isobel.** 1838 to 1884.
    (4) **David.** 1840 to —
    (5) **William.** 1842 to —
    (6) **Mary Ann.** 1846 to —

NOTE.—James, a merchant in Brechin, was a short, stout, dark complexioned man; he was much respected for quiet amiability; died of jaundice 28th May 1874. His wife, a stout, dark woman, had much energy and industry, and was her husband's counterpart for kindly amiability; she died of bronchitis 27th March 1887, aged 84.

(2) **James,** 1836 to — (Table VIII.)

Born 25th Feby.; studied law in Edinburgh; solicitor and banker in Brechin, of the firm of Shiell and Don; married 16th Feby. 1888, **Isabella Brodie** (born 21st May 1849) daughter of Walter Brodie, farmer, Cookston, by his wife Elizabeth Mollison, Chapelton, Dunlappie, and had the following children :—

    (1) **Elizabeth Jane**, 16th Jany. 1869 to —
    (2) **James,** 28th June 1890 to 16th Jany. 1896, a promising boy—died deeply regretted.

(3) **Isobel,** 1838 to 1884.

Lived and died in Brechin—unmarried.

NOTE.—She was an admirable musician.

(4) **David,** 1840 to — (Table VIII.)

Born 13th July; for many years in the Oriental Bank Corporation in India, Africa etc; on its failure, he became manager and liquidator of its estates in South Africa; in 1894, he took over its sugar plantations, in Natal, under a limited company, of which he is Managing Director. Lives in Durban, Natal, and was lately a member of the Legislative Council, which carries the title "Honourable";

married, Sept. 1895, in London, **Marie Nightingale**, of Durban, and has a son.

(1) **David**, 2nd June 1896 to —

(5) **William**, 1842 to — (Table VIII.)

Born 3rd August; an Engineer; sailed as such in the Peninsular and Oriental Company's service; became engineer to the Calcutta Gas Works, and finally settled in that city as a merchant; married in Brechin, 29th July 1896, **Catherine Mary Hodgeton**, daughter of David Hodgeton, chemist, Brechin, by his wife Catherine Lyon Black, whose grandmother was Katherine Don, of Bonnyhard, wife of James Mackie. (Table VI.)

(6) **Mary Ann**, 1846 to —

Born March 30th, married 7th January 1869, **James Young**, Seedsman, Brechin, by whom she had four sons and six daughters. (Table VIII.)

(2) **Thomas**, 1803 to 1878. (Table IX.)

Succeeded his father in business, and in 1852 became farmer in Balzeordie, Menmuir; married 1836, **Ann Low**, and had the following children :

(1) **Catherine** 1837 to

(2) **Margaret** 1840 to

(3) **Andrew Low** 1842 to

(4) **Thomas** 1844 to

(5) **Maria** 1848 to 1873.

(6) **William Carnegie** 1853 to 1877.

(7) **Alexander** 1855 to

(1) **Catherine** 1837 to — (Table IX.)

Married, 1861, **William Swan**, farmer, Moatmill and Balhungie, who died in 1890, and had seven sons and two daughters. (Table IX.)

(2) **Margaret** 1840 to —

Married, 1863, **E. D. Nicol**, merchant of Arbroath and Sunderland, and had six sons and one daughter. (Table IX.)

(3) **Andrew Low** 1842 to — (Table IX.)

Went to London, 1863, as a Linen Agent, in the City; of the

firm of Andrew L. Don & Co. Married, 1869, **Annie Hendrey**, and has the following children :

    (1) **Thomas,** 1870 to
    (2) **Annie,** 1873 to
    (3) **Andrew Chalmers,** 1877 to
    (4) **William Hendrey,** 1883 to
    (5) **Arthur Durran,** 1884 to

(1) **Thomas,** 1870 to —
In his father's business ; unmarried.

(3) **Andrew Chalmers** 1877 to
Student in Divinity.
The rest are at home.

(4) **Thomas** 1844 to —   (Table IX.)

Went to London 1883 ; joined his brother's firm. Married, 1879, **Annie Brown,** and has the following children :

    (1) **Annie,** 1881 to —
    (2) **David,** 1883 to —
    (3) **George Thomas,** 1885 to —
    (4) **Edith Jane,** 1887 to —
    (5) **Mary Catherine,** 1891 to —

(5) **Maria,** 1848 to 1873, unmarried. Suffered from lung affection, and died at the Station Hotel, Carlisle, while on her way to the south of England ; very deeply regretted ; she was remarkable for good looks.

(6) **William Carnegie,** 1853 to 1877, unmarried. Bred a farmer ; emigrated to America 1875 ; died, after three days' illness of scarlet fever in 1877 ; buried at Quincey, Adams Co., Iowa, U.S.A.

(7) **Alexander,** 1855 to —
Bred a seedsman at Drummond's in Stirling ; went to New York, 1883 ; now of the firm of Webber & Don, seedsmen, in that city.

Married 18— **Emma Lee,** and has two sons and two daughters.

    (1) **Alexander.**
    (2) **David.**
    (3) **Alice Gordon.**
    (4) **Annie Low.**

NOTE.—Thomas of Balzeordie, retired from the farm in 1872, and resided in Carnoustie till his death in 1878 ; and was buried in

Brechin. He was a fair complexioned, middle-sized man; of great energy and industry; or, as a friend of his described him to me, 'always busy, often in a hurry'; he was much respected for innate kindness and absolute integrity.

(3) **John**, 1805 to — (Table X.)

Born 16th November, merchant, banker; long a Town Councillor, and quondam Bailie of Brechin. Living in Brechin aged 92. Married, 1831, **Jane Davidson**, who died, deeply regretted, 26th April, 1846, aged 39, and had the following children:

    (1) **Mary Anne**, 1832 to —
    (2) **John Davidson**, 1834 to —
    (3) **Jane Anne**, 1836 to —
    (4) **James**, 1838 to 1849.
    (5) **Charles**, 1843 to 1876.
    (6) **David**, 1844 to 1848.

(1) **Mary Anne**, 1832 to —

Living in Brechin—unmarried.

(2) **John Davidson**, 1834 to — (Table X.)

Educated in Edinburgh; ordained a minister of the Free Church of Scotland in 1858; connected for a number of years with the Free Church College, Calcutta; afterwards of King William's Town, South Africa, where he now resides. Married (1) **Kate Baylie**, and had the following children:

    (1) **John Baylie**, 1864 to —
    (2) **Marion Lanfear**, 1870 to —
    (3) **Kate Neville**, 1871 to —

(1) **John Baylie**, 1864 to —

An engineer; already distinguished as an African explorer—unmarried.

(2) **Marion Lanfear**, 1870 to —

Married, **William Way**, 1894.

John, married, (2), **C. Brownlee**, and has children:

    (1) **Agnes**.
    (2) **Alexander Brownlee**.
    (3) **Isabella Mary**.
    (4) **Jean Dorothy**.

(3) **Jean Anne**, 1836 to — (Table X.)
Married, 1864, **James M. Ross**, Brewer, Montrose, and has the following children :—
       (1) **Margaret**, 1865 to —
       (2) **John**, 1867 to —
       (3) **Anna**, 1871 to —

(4) **Charles**, 1843 to 1876. (Table X.)
Bred a Banker, and served as such in China. Succeeded his father as Agent of the City of Glasgow Bank, Brechin, 1872; married 1874, **Bessie Anderson** of Dundee, and had two sons :—
       (1) **Robert Anderson**, 1875 to — (Now in Bombay).
       (2) **Charles**, 1876 to — (Now in Dundee).

NOTE.—Charles died, 2nd August 1876, of an acute affection of the bowels, after a few hours' illness. His sudden and early death was deeply mourned; and the utmost sympathy was expressed for his young widow, who gave birth to a posthumous son a few days after his death. Personally, he was short, stout, comely; with a profusion of fair hair and beard. His excellent business habits marked him for a career of much usefulness had he been spared. There never was a more loveable, genial fellow; I loved him even as my own younger brother!

(5) **Anne**, 1810 to 1889. (Tables VII. and IX.)
Married **Robert Don**, of whom hereafter.

(6) **Mary**, 1816 to —
Living in Brechin, unmarried.

Chapter VIII.

THE BONNYHARD DONS.

HESE Dons sprang from Alexander by his second wife. They are so named from a farm in Edzell, variously called Balnahard, Bonhard, Bonnyhard; the first is the true Celtic name, meaning 'the town of the high ground'; the second is a phonetic shortening of the first; the third arises from the l being mute, Ba-na-hard—softened to Bonnyhard, and is the best familiar name.

In 1731, (Table III.) **Alexander** married **Janet Leighton**, (my father called her Margaret), who, according to A. Fairweather (commenting on the following entry in the Menmuir Session Record), was widow of John Fairweather:

'4th June 1728, Janet Leighton, spouse of the late John Fair-
'weather, in Inishewan, had a lawful daughter baptized named
' Margaret.'

'Inishewan,' he adds, 'is in Tameadice, but such a record in
' Menmuir Session Books, shows they both had belonged to the
' latter parish originally: very probably, the widow had returned to
' her relatives after the death of her husband,' (and there given birth
' to a posthumous child). 'Query? could the widow have been the
' Janet Leighton, who, on 11th July 1731, was married to Alexander
' Don as his second wife?'

I think there cannot be a doubt of it: married women according to Scottish custom, are legally designated by their maiden names even after marriage.

She bore to Alexander two children:—

   (1) **David**, 1733 to — (Tables III. and VI.)
   (2) **Janet**, 1735 to —

NOTE.—According to the Brechin Register of Marriages 3, **Janet** married **Alexander Smith**, farmer Pitpollux, now Broomfield, on 30th April 1747, an evident mistake for 1757; as the bride would only have been twelve at the former date. A. Fairweather, thought her husband's name was Alexander Fairweather; but he was here mistaken. She had no recorded children.

(1) **David,** 1733 to — (Table VI. Edzell Marriages 6). Married, 19th July 1760, **Jean Henderson,** heiress of the life rent of Bonnyhard; and thus stepped into a ready made home. By her he had the following recorded children :—

    (1) **Alexander,** 1762 to —
    (2) **Elizabeth,** 1764 to —
    (3) **Katherine,** 1766 to —
    (4) **Margaret,** 1767 to —
    (5) **David,** 1770 to —
    (6) **Anne,** 1772 to —

NOTE.—I have no account personally, of the first David of Bonnyhard.

(1) **Alexander,** 1762 to — (Table VI.)

Farmer, Priestown, Dunlappie; married, 1785, **Agnes Smart,** (Edzell Marriages 7) and had the following children :—

    (1) **David,** 1787 to 1865.
    (2) **Isabella,** 1790 to —
    (3) **Alexander Duncan,** 1793 to 1869.
    (4) **Jean,** 1795 to —
    (5) **Betty,** 1797 to —

NOTE.—I have no further record of Alexander of Priestown—a farm since absorbed into another.

(1) **David,** 1787 to 1865.

A Farmer; emigrated to Canada; died unmarried.

(2) **Isabella,** 1790 to—

Married, **William Coutts.** (Table VI.)

(3) **Alexander Duncan.** 1793 to 1869. (Table VI.)

Was in the shoe trade Brechin; married 1821, **Elizabeth Cramond,** and had children :—

    (1) **Isabella,** 1822 to 22.
    (2) **Anne,** 1824 to 81 (unmarried).
    (3) **Margaret,** 1826 to 28.
    (4) **Janet** or **Jessie,** 1829 to —
    (5) **Mary,** 1834—64 (unmarried).
    (6) **Jean,** 1838 to —

(4) **Janet,** 1829 to —

Married, **Alexander Watson.**

(5) **Jean,** 1838 to — (Table VI.)

Born 29th March; living in Manchester. Married, 1861, **Andrew Simpson,** Veterinary Surgeon (born at Coupar Angus 1839) of Fettercairn, and of Kendal, Westmoreland, where he was killed by a fall from his horse 1874 ; she had two sons and five daughters.

(4) **Jean,** 1795 to — (Table VI.)

Married, 1817, (Edzell Marriages 6) **John Smith,** farmer, Dalfouper, Edzell, and had one son and five daughters.

(5) **Betty,** 1797 to —

Married, **John Nicoll,** farmer, Bogburn.

(2) **Elizabeth,** 1764 to —

Married, 1788, **Alexander Duncan,** farmer, Sandyhillocks, Edzell. No children.

(3) **Katherine,** 1766 to — (Table VI.)

Married 1796, **James Mackie,** farmer, Westerton of Balfour, and had children who established a rather wide connection, as follows :—

    (1) **Anne,** 1797 to — (M. James Black).

    (2) **Jean,** 1800 to — (M. James Crabb).

    (3) **James,** 1802 to 1881 (farmer Thornyhill M. E. Lindsay).

    (4) **David,** 1803 to — (Died in infancy).

    (5) **Betsy,** ⎱ 1806 to — ⎰ (M. John Lindsay).

    (6) **Margaret,** ⎰ (twins) ⎱ (M. David Edwards).

    (7) **John,** 1809 to 1889. (Doctor of Medicine Brechin, married, Mary Ann Black).

(4) **Margaret,** 1797 to —

Married, 1805, (Edzell Marriages 10) **John Anderson,** Marykirk, and had a daughter.

(6) **Anne,** 1772 to —

Married, 1807, (Edzell Marriages 11) **Robert Watson,** Gannochy. No children.

F

(5) **David**, 1770 to 1818? (Table VI., Edzell Marriages 12, Straecathro Marriages 6.)

'Married, 1807, his cousin, **Christian Hood**, and had a son :—
  (1) **David**, 1809 to —

NOTE.—I have no record of this David's wife's name, or children, if any : but I recollect him visiting Ballownie, as late as 1845. He lived at Stonehaven, and with him the Bonnyhard Dons became extinct in the male line.

NOTE.—David, the last farmer of Bonnyhard, was a character in the neighbourhood, and many stories of his eccentricities have come down. Of these, the following has the merit of being strictly true : When Christian Hood, died, he bethought him of another cousin as a second wife—Mary Don of Ballownie, and made a ludicrous attempt to court her. In the spirit and style of the Laird of Cockpen, he rode to Ballownie, where he was cordially received by my father, and taken 'ben.' David at once confided the object of his visit, soliciting my father's good offices as an intermediary, but such delicate business was at once declined. At this juncture Mary herself, unsuspiciously came upon the scene; on which my father attempted escape, but was stopped by David, with, 'Sit down, 'Ballownie, we've nae secrets here.' Without further parley, and ignoring my father's presence, he began : 'Ye ken, Mary, I've been 'thinkin' I want some ane to fill Kirsty's place ; you and her waur 'guid freends, an' ye wad be kind till her bairn ; and,' (after an awkward pause, throwing out his arms, continued in the most winning accents) 'and I've been thinkin', how weel I wad lie i' the 'Kirkyard atween ye baith, wi ane in ilka arm !'

For a moment taken aback, Mary then firmly replied : 'Na, na, 'Bonnyhard, I dinna intend to marry ava '; and whisked out of the room.

Bonnyhard mounted his mare and rode home 'cannily'; he never remarried ; a lonely and somewhat unsteady life soon finished him. Mary also, kept her word ; and lived to be in the estimation of a host of nephews and nieces the very perfection of a maiden aunt.

CHAPTER IX.

THE BALLOWNIE DONS.

THE FARM of Ballownie, Stracathro, which gives name to this section of the Dons, is, judging from its name, perhaps the oldest homestead in the parish; for those surrounding it nearly all bear later Anglo-Saxon names. Its Celtic etymology is, *bal*, town; *lownie*, meadowy place; that is, the homestead of the meadows, or the haughs on the river Cruick. It is not only ancient, but of much historic interest, from the circumstance that the Roman Road, passing to the Kingsford on the North Esk, bisected it; its situation made it the scene of some memorable events; including the great battle in A.D. 1130 between King David I., and the Maormor of Moray; which was the decisive struggle for supremacy between Saxons and Celts in Scotland; all of which I have related in my 'Archæological Notes on Early Scotland'; published at Brechin, 1896.

At the time when the Dons entered on the farm, November 1742, it was the property of Homer Grierson, Merchant, Brechin; from whom it passed to Speid of Ardovie; and, after my father's day to the present laird, Campbell of Stracathro. It was tenanted by three Alexander Dons, consectively, from 1742 to 1851, a period of 109 years; and must therefore ever have an abiding interest to all their descendants.

I have traced **Alexander** the first, from Blackhall to Ireland, and now follow him to Ballownie. He had married his second wife, Janet Leighton, about 1731; but matrimonial misfortune stuck to him, and he lost her between 1740-44; but whether before or after entering on Ballownie I cannot say. At all events, at Ballownie he was a widower for the second time, with two young families on his hands. His thrifty and sympathetic women neighbours, having noticed, among other evidences of the want of a guidwife, cold porridge floating down the stream, warned him: "Sandy Don, gin " ye dinna sune tak anither wife, your servants will waste ye oot o' " hoose and ha'."

Consequently, on 21st January 1745 (Table III. Brechin Marriages 2), he married his third wife, **Janet Prophet**, whose father lived near the Roman Camp at the Blackdykes; from her descended the Ballownie Dons, as follows:

I. Family.

(1) **Alexander**, 1746 to 1808.
(2) **Cathren**, 1748 to —
(3) **Jean**, 1751 to —
(4) **Christian**, 1753 to —

Before tracing these children I will finish the history of their parents.

NOTE.—Alexander ran two nineteen years' leases on Ballownie, of which the latter part of the second passed to his son Alexander. He died 1779, aged 79, at Ballownie, and was buried with his fathers in Menmuir. I have heard him personally spoken of as strong, wiry, and fresh or fair complexioned. I have seen his signature, bold and firm, to a will (see Appendix II.). He was industrious, very independent, and a strong Whig, as the following story, told by my father, shows. Alexander, being a firm 'Hanoverian,' and Presbyterian, was of course obnoxious to the Jacobites of the rebellion of 1745; when it broke out a detachment of the Highland Host, marching south to join Prince Charlie at Perth, passed Ballownie, and sent a picket to the farm threatening the Whig with fire and sword unless he sent a man to their ranks; for, by such tactics they not only swelled the fighting force of the Clansmen, but hoped to compromise as many anti-Jacobite lowlanders as possible. He could only comply; but gave his servant a hint to desert on the first opportunity, which he managed to embrace before they reached Perth. Next year, April 1746, the rebellion was cruelly stamped out on the bloody field of Calloden, and all rebels, real or suspected, taken to task; in September of the same year, Alexander, the second, was born. At that time there was a vacancy in the Church of Stracathro, and the infant had to be carried to the adjoining parish of Pert for baptism; but before the rite could be administered the really loyal farmer had to undergo formal admonition for his involuntary share in the rebellion, in having sent at least one rebel into the field. "Such," comments my father in 1847, recalling no doubt recollection of the Jacobite politics of his young days, "was the zeal of the Presbyterian clergy in favour of the *existing* Government."

This curious incident gives us a glimpse of the fierce controversies which then convulsed Scotland : politics now to us dead—dead ; also of the enthusiasm, devotion and sacrifice of our grandsires, for a mere sentiment ; beside them, we, in these prosaic days, seem almost incapable of heroics !

Of Janet Prophet, the chief peculiarity lies in her name ; it is limited to, and very rare in north east Scotland, and sometimes of the spelling Profeit, (as Dr. Profeit, late Queen's Commissioner at Balmoral). It may be Huguenot, of the spelling Prophéte. But our grand dame, good Janet, had nothing French about her ; for she was of the true Saxo-Scandinavian type ; sonsie, ruddy, fair, solid and stolid. She died at Ballownie, 1799, aged 80 years, and was buried in Stracathro ; not in the present Don's enclosure, but in the line of the walk now passing to the left of the entrance gate ; so that, Sunday by Sunday, several generations of worshippers have unconsciously passed over the last resting-place of good old Janet.

With these two ancestors the old order of things passed away, and a new era fairly commenced in Scotland, which has led to the marvellous results we note in the present day. On this I shall afterwards comment (Appendix I.).

The following is the record of the daughters of Alexander and Janet Prophet.

(2) **Cathren**, 1748 to — (Table III. Stracathro Baptisms 2, Marriages 2). Married, 1778, **Alexander Stoole**, farmer, Milldens, Stracathro ; and had four sons, and two daughters, all extinct.

NOTE.—The last was James Stoole, schoolmaster, and teacher of navigation, Deptford, Kent, who died 1853. I can remember his visiting Ballownie ; a stout, garrulous man, full of naval tales, which filled me with wonder ; he brought presents of snuff-boxes, made from recovered oak of the famous 'Royal George,' sunk at Spithead in 1782.

(3) **Jean**, 1751 to — (Stracathro Baptisms 3, Marriages 1). Twice married, without children : (1) 1773 to **Robert Goldie** ; (2) 1789 to ˙**David Fettes** (Edzell Marriages 9).

(4) **Christian**, 1753 to — (Stracathro Marriages 4) Married, 1788, **William Hood**, farmer, Syde of Stracathro, and had three sons and three daughters, the last being Janet, drowned in the river Cruick, 1869.

II. Family.

(1) **Alexander**, 1746 to 1808 (Tables III and XI, Stracathro Baptisms 1, Marriages 3). Succeeded his father as second in Ballownie ; married 8th December, 1775, **Jean Hood**, daughter of John Hood, farmer, Syde, Stracathro ; the sister of William Hood, who married Christian Don, thereby establishing a double family connection. Their children were :

    (1) **Jean**, 7th January 1777 to 2nd March 1854.
    (2) **Jannet**, 11th Aug. 1778 to   1805.
    (3) **John**, 3rd March 1781 to   1808.
    (4) **Alexander**, 19th Novr. 1782 to 10th Novr. 1850.
    (5) **David**, 5th July 1784 to 25th Dec. 1863.
    (6) **Mary**, 23rd May 1786 to 6th Oct. 1861.
    (7) **Robert**, 5th Feby. 1788 to 17th April 1853.
    (8) **Thomas**, 11th April 1790 to   1821.
    (9) **William**, 1st July 1791 to 28th Jany. 1850.
    (10) **Hannah**, 22nd Oct. 1793 to   1804.
    (11) **James**, (1) 10th Decr. 1795 to   1796.
    (12) **James**, (2) 10th Sepr. 1798 to 24th July 1864.

NOTE.—Alexander died 1808 (from so-called dysentery) ; and was buried in Stracathro. He had long been a ruling Elder in the parish, and on his death, the Revd. Robert Hanna, Minister, wrote a highly eulogistic, albeit patronizing letter, on the virtues of his deceased parishioner. He was indeed, a man of high integrity ; simple and inoffensive ; but very sociable and fond of conviviality. I have heard him described as of middle height, spare and fair, with grey or hazel eyes.

Jean Hood, survived him thirty years, and died March 1838, aged 82 years. She was a woman of striking personal qualities ; tall, stately, dignified ; dark complexioned, with fine black eyes ; characteristics largely transmitted in her children ; her temperament was very placid and disposition warm and affectionate. She was buried in Stracathro.

(1) **Jean**, 1777 to 1854. (Stracathro Baptisms 4, Marriages 5.) Married, 1798, **David Webster**, farmer, Mill of Balrownie and had four sons and six daughters ; namely: (Table XI.) James 1799-1875, banker, and factor to the Duke of Hamilton, unmarried ; Alexander, 1801-78, farmer, Muirside of Balzeordie, unmarried ; David, 1803-72, farmer, Blackhall and Mill of Balrownie, unmarried ; Jean, 1805-87, married James Don, Brechin (Table VIII.). Janet, 1807, died young ; Elizabeth 1809, died young ; Mary 1811-87, married Joseph Taylor and had issue : Annie 1813, unmarried ; William 1815-58, farmer, Mill of Balrownie, unmarried ; Isabella 1819, married 1851, David Fairweather, farmer, Laughaugh, and had, Jean Ann, Isabella, David, John and Elizabeth Mary.

NOTE.—Jean much resembled her mother physically and mentally ; she was buried in Menmuir. Her husband was of a race of typical Scottish farmers ; his father was James Webster of Balrownie, his mother, Elizabeth Scott. James, who died in 1812, aged 84, was a clever, industrious man, proved by the fact that he placed seven sons in farms ; his aptitude in making money, and fine faculty in holding his own, earned him the funny and punning nickname,—' King A-grip-a ' !

(2) **Jannet**, 1778 to 1805. (Stracathro Baptisms 5.) Died unmarried.

(3) **John**, 1781 to 1808. (Stracathro Baptisms 6.) Died of pneumonia, at Ballownie, unmarried.

NOTE.—He was a man 6 ft. 4 in., gigantic in stature and strength, the tallest of a very tall family ; yet, in gentleness and geniality, a little child. He was an excellent mimic and very droll ; his early death was much lamented.

I omit for the present, Alexander, my father, who comes next.

(5) **David**, 1784 to 1863. (Stracathro Baptisms 9). Became farmer, Keirsbeith, Fife, about 1815. Married, **Elizabeth Hogg,** of Kinross, and had :

    (1) **David**, Jany. 1818 to 1855.
    (2) **Lillias**, Aug. 1820 to 1825.
    (3) **Alexander**, Jany. 1822 to 1883.
    (4) **James**, March 1824 to 1854.
    (5) **Jane Hood**, Feby. 1827 to —

(1) **David**, 1818 to 1855.

A merchant at Gateshead and Newcastle-on-Tyne, died unmarried.

NOTE.—He was a stout, good looking, burly man ; of great kindness and heartiness.

(2) **Lillias**, 1820 to 1825.

Died from the effects of a severe scald.

(3) **Alexander**, 1822 to 1883.

Succeeded his father in Keirsbeith ; died unmarried.

NOTE.—Was a very stout, hearty open-faced man ; and considered one of the best auctioneers and valuers of farm produce in the kingdom of Fife : he died of paralysis.

(4) **James**, 1824 to 1854.

Died, unmarried, at Kiersbeith.

NOTE.—Was a very warmed-hearted, big, stout man.

(5) **Jane Hood** 1827 to —

Married, 1847, **John Frederick Smith**, of the '*Caledonian Mercury*' newspaper, Edinburgh, who died of fever, while yet a fine young man, in 1849, leaving two daughters. Eliza Bell, and Joanna Jane, the latter born posthumous, July, 1849, married 1877, Alexander Don. (Table XI).

NOTE.—David of Keirsbeith, was of great stature; when over seventy I can recall him towering above his fellows in the streets of Edinburgh. He was one of a guard of Fife Yeomen, provided for George IV. when he visited Holyrood, in 1822 ; it is said the king stared at Trooper Don, and remarked; 'Why, he beats the Life Guards!' I knew him as an old man, with large brown eyes, ruddy face, and shock head of snow white hair. In his heyday his social qualities were of the first order ; the life of every company with anecdote and song ! His wife died 8th March, 1858, aged 68.

(6) **Mary**, 1786 to 1861. (Stracathro Baptisms 11).

Died in Brechin 6th Oct., 1861, unmarried, buried in Stracathro.

NOTE.—Dear Auntie Mary ! Like her mother, tall, stately, dignified ; faultless in dress ; but absolutely without pride or affectation, and full to overflowing with tenderness and kindness ; the ideal maiden aunt ; adored by her very numerous nephews and nieces.

(7) **Robert** 1788 to 1853 (Table IX. Stracathro Baptisms 12).

Carpenter builder in Brechin; married 7th March, 1834, **Anne Don** (Table VII.), and had ;
- (1) **Mary Carnegie** 28th July, 1835 to —
- (2) **Alexander** 17th May, 1837 to —
- (3) **William Carnegie** 21st Dec., 1839 to 26th Jany., 1848.

(1) **Mary Carnegie** 1835 to —

Living in Brechin—unmarried.

(2) **Alexander** 1837 to —

Bred a banker, in Brechin, Edinburgh and Glasgow; went to India 1864, and was Agent of the Bank of Bombay at Ajmere and Dharwar; lived in India about twelve years, finally returning home in July, 1877, and becoming Inspector, Royal Bank of Scotland, a position he still holds in Edinburgh. Married 25th Oct., 1877, **Joanna Jane Smith**, his cousin, once removed, and had children.
- (1) **Frederick Alexander**, Nov. 14th, 1878 to —
- (2) **Norman Robert**, Decr. 1885 to July 7th, 1886.
- (3) **Henry William**, April 8th, 1887 to —
- (4) **Ida Mary**, April 7th, 1889 to —

(3) **William Carnegie**, 1839 to 1848.

A pretty, gentle boy. Died of scarlet fever.

NOTE.—Robert died suddenly, probably of heart disease, in church, Sunday, April 17th, 1853, under impressive circumstances, which caused much sensation in Brechin. He was an Elder in the East Free Church, and stood by the church door plate, on the afternoon of his death, apparently in his usual health; after the service had begun he went to his pew, and while engaged in singing Psalm 73, Verse 23 :

> 'Nevertheless, continually'
> 'O Lord, I am with thee'

his head sunk on the open book and he immediately expired! Next Sunday, the Revd. J. E. Carlisle, preached a funeral sermon from the text,

> 'He will swallow up death in victory,'

and remarked, Robert Don was perhaps the most guileless and lovable Christian he ever met. His old minister, the famous Revd. Dr. McCosh, then a Professor in Belfast, wrote a touching letter to the bereaved widow, from which these extracts :—

'Belfast, 21st April, 1853 . . . I looked upon your late 'husband, as one of the best and steadiest friends I had acquired on 'earth . . . . He did good by his prayers; his deeds; by his 'consistent upright character; by his stedfast unflinching principles. ' Every recollection I have of your departed husband is mingled with 'nothing unworthy. . . . I desire to mingle my tears with yours.'

He was highly esteemed in Brechin, of which city he had long been a Councillor, and where, literally, he had no enemy. I can still see his tall stooping figure; benevolent face; mild brown eyes; and shock head of white hair; and can hear the soft musical voice of the man I loved next to my own father! He was buried in Brechin parish churchyard. His wife, a fair blue-eyed woman, much beloved, died Decr. 19th, 1889, and was also buried in Brechin.

(8) **Thomas** 1790 to 1821 (Stracathro Baptisms 13).

A cabinet maker; a man of much mechanical genius, but prolonged ill-health from lung disease, unfitted him for any regular work. My mother described him as singularly skilful with his hands; and of a disposition exceedingly gentle and amiable. He died unmarried, and was buried in Stracathro.

(9) **William,** 1791 to 1850 (Stracathro Baptisms 14).

A mason builder; settled in Montreal, Canada, as a marble cutter. Married, 1827, **Agnes McIntosh,** who died 1876. Their children constitute a group of **American Dons.**

    (1) **Jane,** 1828 to 1832.
    (2) **Robert,** 1829 to —
    (3) **Alexander,** 1831 to —
    (4) **William,** (1) 1833 to 1835.
    (5) **James,** 1834 to 1875.
    (6) **David,** 1836 to —
    (7) **William,** (2) 1838 to —
    (8) **Agnes Mary,** 1840 to 1844.
    (9) **Elizabeth Wright,** 1843 to 1878.
    (10) **Thomas,** 1845 to 1846.
    (11) **Mary Jean,** 1847 to 1847.

(2) **Robert**, 1829 to —

Formerly in business ; now lives on private means, in Davenport, Iowa. Married 1886, **Ottilie Dorothea Johanna Graaek**, born in Germany, 1859; no children.

(3) **Alexander**, 1831 to —

In the hardware trade at Rock Island, U.S.A., with his brother David ; unmarried.

(5) **James**, 1834 to 1875.

In business, Rock Island, U.S.A. Married 1868, **Maggie McGhee**, and had children :
- (1) **William S.**, 1869 to 1895.
- (2) **Gussie**, 1872 to 1890.
- (3) **Agnes**, 1874 to 1891.

James died in 1875 ; and his family are also extinct.

(6) **David**, 1836 to —

In the hardware trade, Rock Island. Married, July 1st, 1874, **Agnes Jackson**, Davenport, Iowa, and had the following children :
- (1) **Louington**, 1875 to 1876.
- (2) **David**, 1877 to 1877.
- (3) **Elizabeth Gertrude**, 1882 to —
- (4) **Elbert**, 1885 to —
- (5) **De Forest**, 1886 to —
- (6) **Irene Constance**, 1888 to —

(7) **William**, 1838 to —

In the book and bookbinding trade, Davenport, Iowa ; unmarried.

(9) **Elizabeth Wright**, 1843 to 1878.

Married, 1874, **James T. Dixon** ; no surviving descendants.

NOTE.—For the foregoing information on the American Dons I am indebted to Robert, of Davenport, Iowa. I have little to record of his father William ; I have heard him described as strongly resembling his worthy brothers Robert and Thomas.

(10) **Hannah**, 1793 to 1804.

Died a girl.

(11) **James**, (1) 1795 to 1796.

Died an infant.

(12) **James,** (2) 1798 to 1864.

Unmarried. Died at Bearehill, Brechin; buried in Brechin Cemetery, against the north wall; and a granite cenotaph is over his grave.

NOTE.—His career was most honourable. Left a boy of ten when his father died, he was brought up and educated for the medical profession, by his eldest surviving brother, my father. He and Dr. Fettes of Laurencekirk were the first, even as I, forty years afterwards, was among the last of the pupils of Alexander Guthrie, Surgeon, Brechin. Studied in Edinburgh and Aberdeen, and graduated in the latter University, Doctor of Medicine in 1824, having some years previously obtained the Diploma of the Royal College of Surgeons of Edinburgh. After several voyages to India and China, he received in 1824, a Commission as Assistant Surgeon in the Honourable East India Company's Service, Bombay Presidency. During a service of thirty three years, he held several important and lucrative appointments, among which were: Vaccinator Khandeish Province; Staff Surgeon Poona; Superintending Surgeon, Scinde; and Surgeon General of the Bombay Medical Board. His health giving way he retired in 1857, just before the outbreak of the Mutiny. Having amassed considerable wealth, he purchased in 1862, the estate of Bearehill, Brechin, where he died, of paralysis, 24th July 1864. By his will he founded the Brechin Infirmary.

He adopted myself when a boy, as his successor in the medical profession, and made me his chief heir.

He was held in the very highest esteem in India, and when I went to Bombay in 1858, as a Staff Assistant Surgeon in the Army, was everywhere received, from the Governor downwards, with much kindest on my uncle's account.

Personally, he was very tall, dark, and of a distinguished bearing; so that in his day, he was pronounced by ladies—'the handsomest man in the Bombay Army.' But with splendid physical endowments, and the most polished manners, he retained complete native unaffectedness and geniality; and clung to his kindred and home with the warmest affection.

There never was one who better merited or sustained the epithet 'Gentleman'; an honor to all his kith and kin, and to myself one to whom I am unspeakably indebted.

III. Family.

Under this head my own father, third in Ballownie, and his family, come to be described.

(4) **Alexander.** 1782 to 1850. (Tables IX. and XII. Stracathro Baptisms 7. Marriages 7).

Succeeded his father in Ballownie, as third of the name; married 22nd July 1820, **Jean Fullerton**, eldest daughter of James Fullerton (See Appendix IV.) farmer Brathinch, Menmuir; by his wife Mary Valentine of Pitgarvie (See Appendix III.), and had the following children :

(1) **Jean Valentine**, 21st July 1821 to 15 Sep. 1855.
(2) **Margaret Fullerton**, 28th Feby. 1823 to —
(3) **James**, 5th Oct. 1825 to   Feby. 1890.
(4) **Alexander**, 8th Feby. 1827 to —
(5) **Henry Speid**, 1st Feby. 1829 to 18th Novr. 1868.
(6) **Robert**, 6th July 1831 to 19th March 1838.
(7) **William Gerard**, 10th Jany. 1836 to —

(1) **Jean.** 1821 to 1855. (Tables XI. and XII.)

Married, July, 1850, her second cousin, **Walter Hood**, Shipbuilder, Aberdeen, and had :

(1) **Jane**, 1851 to 1890.

Married, 1885, Thomas Hillier, Bristol, and had Dorothy, Winnie, Jane and Thomas. She was buried at Clifton Cemetery.

(2) **John**, 1853 to —

Married in Australia, Jane Penman, and has a numerous family living near Bristol.

NOTE.—Jean, died after a long illness following the birth of her son John; buried in Nellfield Cemetery, Aberdeen.

She was short, stout and ruddy; of a temperament so even that none ever saw her angry; a being most placid, guileless and unselfish; never could there be a more lovable daughter, sister or wife; she was my guardian angel when I was a child.

Her husband, Walter Hood, was a portly powerful man; distinguished as the builder of the famous Aberdeen Clippers, of the forties and fifties, in the firms of Walter Hood & Co. and George Thompson, Jr. & Co., Aberdeen and London. He was a much respected citizen of Aberdeen, and lost his life by falling into the dock, on Christmas Eve, 1862; his body was brought to the surface only by the firing of cannon over the water; was buried in Nellfield.

(2) **Margaret.** 1823 to — (Tables XI. and XII.)

Married, 1849, **James Elder**, Flour Merchant, Liverpool, a dark, fine looking man, from Leven in Fife, who died 1869, aged 57. Her children were :

    (1) **Jane**, 1850 to 1852.

    (2) **Janet Bruce**, 1852 to 1867; died at Fettercairn and was buried in Stracathro.

    (3) **James**, 1853, married, with children, in Liverpool.

    (4) **Helen Scott**, 1856, married to John Mackay, Liverpool, and has issue.

    (5) **Margaret**, 1857 to — married Robert H. Mather, Glasgow, and has a son.

    (6) **Mary Don**, 1859 to — married Timothy Warren, Writer, Glasgow, and has eight sons and daughters.

    (7) **Christian Anderson**, 1861 to 1889, unmarried.

NOTE.—Christian died of fever while a Nurse in St. Mary's Hospital, London, 22nd July, 1889; buried in Hamilton Cemetery. A woman, handsome, amiable beloved in no ordinary degree; my dearest ' Kirsty,' whom I regarded as my own daughter !

(3) **James**, 1825 to 1890. (Tables XI. and XII.)

Studied law first, and then divinity in Edinburgh and Aberdeen. Licensed a Minister of the Free Church of Scotland, 1852; held officiating charges at Crathie, Channel Islands and Wick; sent to Australia by the Colonial Committee of the Church in 1857; held charges in Penola and Mount Gambier, South Australia, and finally settled in the Presbyterian Church at Kyneton, Victoria, where he died, February, 1890, and was buried.

Twice married; first, to **Zelia Lauga**, of Guernsey, a lady of Franco-Spanish extraction, by whom he formed a group of **Australian Dons;** the following were their children :—

    (1) **Harriet Jane**, 1858 to 1895.

Married, the Rev. **Alexander McConnan**, Victoria, and had six children, dying with the last, deeply regretted.

NOTE.—Unfortunately I do not have the names of her children. She was the only one of James's family I had seen; a handsome, dark woman, resembling both her parents; she had a beautiful mezzo-soprano voice.

   (2) **Mary,** 1861 to — married J. Pringle.

   (3) **James William,** 1863 to — unmarried.

   (4) **Henry,** 1865 to — unmarried.

   (5) **Margaret,** 1867 to — married.

   (6) **Alexander,** 1869 to — unmarried.

 These sons, as far as I know, are in various occupations in Australia and India.

 Zelia Lauga, died 1877, aged 47; James married as his second wife, **Isabella Powstie,** originally from Greenock; and had children :—

   (1) **Horace,** 1881 to —

   (2) **Gertrude,** 1883 to —

 His widow lives in Kyneton.

 Note.—James's peculiar personality, is lovingly cherished by his family and friends. He was strong, square, spare, of middle height, very active and muscular; large head and face; dark eyes, black hair and beard. He was, by temperament, essentially a poet, and wrote some pretty sonnets; which side of his nature made him as a preacher more flowery than dialectic; but his sermons were always elegant in composition, for he had much literary ability and facility; while his penmanship was so excellent that his manuscripts could be read like print. He had a curious double character; now very absent-minded, silent and self-absorbed; anon, loquacious, monopolizing conversation in inimitable story telling and anecdote; when in the mood few could rival him as a raconteur, or a mimic and caricaturist of public and local characters. His reveries sometimes went great lengths, as in the following instance : When a student at Ballownie, he set out one day for a walk, and went on and on, in a brown study, until confronted with the sea ten miles from home; aroused, he simply turned and tramped back, unconcerned; for his activity in those days made light of a twenty mile stretch. But although unpractical; his guileless amiability won the hearts and the confidence of all with whom he came in contact.

(4) **Alexander**, 1827 to —

Merchant and bank agent, Fettercairn; married, 1872, his maternal cousin, **Jane Ann Ross**, youngest daughter of George Ross, Distiller, Brechin, by whom he had the following children:—

    (1) **Anne Fullerton**, 1872 to —
    (2) **Jean**, 1874 to 1875.
    (3) **Alexander**, 1876 to —
    (4) **John**, 1878 to 1878.
    (5) **William**, 1879 to —
    (6) **Margaret**, 1880 to —
    (7) **Christian**, 1882 to 1883.
    (8) **Alice**, 1884 to 1885.

(3) **Alexander**, 1876 to —
Bred a farmer.

(5) **William**, 1879 to —
In his father's business.

(5) **Henry Speid**, 1829 to 1868.

Unmarried. Died at Galle Face Hotel, Ceylon, 18th November, 1868, of dysentery; buried there.

NOTE.—Bred a farmer; managed Ballownie during his father's infirm years, and ought to have succeeded him. After managing farms in Ireland and England, he went to Ceylon as a coffee planter, 1858, and, in partnership with David Soutar, cleared a fine estate near Happotelle; which was named "Arnhall," after Soutar's Edzell birthplace. When about to reap the advantage of their enterprise, first Henry, and then Soutar, died; and the estate, worth £30,000, was seized by the Ceylon Company, by foreclosure of a small mortgage, and was thus entirely lost to the proper heirs; (the Ceylon Company went to the dogs immediately after this undoubted piece of sharp practice).

Henry's premature death was a source of much grief, especially to his mother, of whom he was a favourite son. In person he stood nearly six feet, stout, and broad, but looked shorter from a habit of stooping; he was sallow and dark, and although powerful physically, had not a strong constitution. He possessed such versatility and capacity that, with life and opportunity, was fitted for almost any sphere. He possessed all the literary ability of his brother James;

but, unlike him, was intensely practical : no work with head or hands seemed to come amiss to him. He was a most amusing companion, full of fun and frolic, but was somewhat masterful and overbearing. In Ceylon he was recognized as a good all-round man ; whether in business, in sport, in editing the ' Planter's Gazette,' or as a boon companion ; and went by the name of ' Clever Henry Don.'

(6) **Robert**, 1831 to 1838.

A very handsome and intelligent boy ; died of scarlet fever.

(7) **William Gerard**, 1836 to —

(The present writer, who will be pardoned the *Ego* in an autobiographic sketch).

Became, 1850, a pupil of Alexander Guthrie, Surgeon, Brechin ; studied medicine in Edinburgh ; a Licentiate of the Royal College of Surgeons of Edinburgh, 1856 ; Doctor of Medicine in the University, 1857. Volunteered, 1855, in response to the Government, for the Baltic Fleet ; and served as a "Doctor's Mate" in the Flagship "Duke of Wellington," 131 guns; took part in the three days' bombardment of Sveaborg in August of that year—Baltic Medal. (Wrote, in 1894, "Reminiscences of the Baltic Fleet of 1855," printed for private circulation). Entered the then new competition for Commissions in the Army Medical Department, January, 1858, and took first place, among twenty-seven competitors. Went to Bombay in August of the same year, and served for six months in Central India in the final suppression of the Mutiny—Medal ; present in the actions, with the rebels under Tantia Topee, at Rajpore and Beilkaira. Served ten years in the 28th Regiment ; six in the Royal Engineers ; two in the Royal Artillery, and nine on the Staff, of which the latter six was in the War Office, London ; foreign service, included India, Bermuda, and the Mediterranean. Retired in 1885, and immediately appointed to the staff of the London Recruiting District, where he has served ever since, or forty years in all. During eighteen years in London, became identified with several—especially Scottish—Societies ; including Honorary Secretary, Edinburgh University Club of London ; President of the Caledonian Society of London, 1894-5 ; on the Management of the Royal Scottish Hospital ; Chairman of the Hamilton Association for the supply of Male Nurses, etc. ; Author of many articles in current literature; of 'Archæological Notes on Early Scotland' published in Brechin, 1896, etc.

Married, June 5th, 1866, at St. Andrew's, Plymouth, **Louisa Jane Elliott**, second daughter of Captain E. G. Elliott, R.N., and had children:—

    (1) **Gilbert Elliott**, 22nd March, 1867 to —
    (2) **Caroline Moore**, 18th November, 1868 to —
    (3) **Mabel Mylius**, 4th November, 1869 to —
    (4) **Gerard Lewin**, 5th October, 1870 to 10th December, 1880.
    (5) **William Walton**, 3rd April, 1872 to —

(1) **Gilbert**, 1867 to —

Unmarried. Educated at Blairlodge School and Glasgow University. For three years in the mercantile house of Wilson, Sons & Co., in Santos and Rio de Janeiro, Brazil. Went to South Africa in 1891; now gold mining in the Transvaal.

(2) **Caroline**, 1868 to —
Unmarried. Living in Natal.

(3) **Mabel**, 1869 to —

Married, 12th June, 1895, **Matthew Robin**, engineer, Glasgow, and has a son:

    (1) **Robert Douglas**, 18th March, 1896 to —

(4) **Gerard**, 1870 to 1880.

Died of scarlet fever, 10th December, 1880, at Hamilton, and buried at the Cemetery there.

NOTE.—A fair, blue-eyed, very handsome, but rather delicate boy; he was very clever, and displayed remarkable powers in caricature drawing; the death of one of such promise was a deep sorrow.

(5) **William**, 1872 to —

Unmarried: studied medicine in Glasgow; graduated there Bachelor, in 1893, and Doctor of Medicine with 'Honours' in 1897. After voyages, as a ship's surgeon, to India, China, Japan, Cape, New Zealand and South America, is now practising in London.

NOTE.—Louisa Jane Elliott, died with her sixth child (stillborn), at Devonport, 16th April, 1874; buried in Stoke Cemetery. Born at Kinsale, Ireland, 23rd November, 1841. She was of middle size, almost a brunette; a woman of the highest principles, quick and humorous, and of affectionate disposition. At the time of her death her husband was in India, and at once returned to place his little children under the care of his widowed sister, Margaret; by whom, they were brought up, with her own family, with the utmost solicitude and care, at Hamilton near Glasgow.

William married, 26th June, 1889, his second wife, **Jean Ann Fairweather,** his paternal cousin removed, daughter of David Fairweather, farmer, Laughaugh, and Isabella Webster, his wife, and had two children, a son stillborn, 1891, and :

(1) **David Fairweather,** 23rd August, 1893 to —

NOTE.—My own revered father, Alexander, third and last on Ballownie, died 10th November, 1850, and was buried in Stracathro. Well do I remember that Sunday night, when my mother, brothers (sisters were absent), and uncle Robert, gathered around the bed to see him die ! When I, his Benjamin and pet, felt I could have laid down my own boyish life to save one I loved so dearly ! He had qualities of head and heart which commanded the affection and respect of all who knew him. Although his early education had been limited, his native intelligence and self cultivation raised him mentally much above his contemporaries, in his station of life; he was a great reader, deeply versed in history; and cultivated a literary style and correctness of diction rare among his fellows. He was, moreover, in breadth of view, fairness and tolerance a philosopher, ahead of his day; no man was less of a bigot or zealot. Yet, although studious, he was no recluse, but fond of company, and, as an admirable story teller and singer, put life into any gathering. Especially did he shine in the glorious naval songs of his day, of which he knew more than any one I have met; notwithstanding that he had no knowledge of sea life, and was a pure landsman. But his contemplative cast of mind ill assorted with success as a farmer; so he died poor, but nevertheless perfectly content. He was intellectually drawn to join the Free Church at the Disruption, no doubt against his naturally Conservative instincts; for, severance from the Church of his fathers, of which he had long been a ruling Elder, and as such the friend and confidant of all in the parish, must have been much against his inclinations; he was an Elder of the Free Church at Edzell, until his death. That was indirectly the result of an accident on 10th August, 1846, of which my sister Margaret and I were the helpless witnesses; in endeavouring to catch one of several horses in a field, he was, in a stampede, thrown and kicked; when we raised him up, his right leg was found fractured, as well as several of his ribs and chest bone; he was borne home on a door by harvesters, almost dead from shock; yet, he slowly recovered, and was able to ride about on a pony. In 1849, gangrene of the toes of the injured leg set in; yet he recovered even from that disease after months of intense suffering. But his fine constitution was now shattered, and he finally succumbed to paralysis.

Personally, he was much the shortest of a very tall family; but was nevertheless, of middle height, strong, broad, clean made and very active. His head was exceptionally massive, so that he always had to get his hats specially made; face ruddy, eyes brown, hair black; a very decided tendency to gout, enforced habits of temperance.

I am here tempted to describe his dress, which, generally, would equally picture all the larger farmers of his day and district; it is well, moreover, to record peculiarities in attire of past days, which are only too apt to fade out of recollection.

Coat, bottle-green, or black, broad tailed with large back or side pockets; neck high.

Waistcoat, sometimes flowered, and generally dandy.

Trousers, dark, rather tight, sometimes with straps.

Shoes with black or buff spats.

Shirt collars, stiff, high, tied behind.

Stock, large, deep necked, of satin or silk.

Hat, tall, black or white, of silk or beaver.

Great coat or 'top coat,' ample, sometimes tippetted.

My father's dress or habits never varied; he took snuff freely, from a silver mounted deer-horn mull, which habit necessitated a huge turkey red handkerchief, carried either in the capacious coat pockets, or in crown of the hat; he was never seen abroad without a 'staff,' or a big whale-bone ribbed umbrella.

He was buried in the grave of his gigantic brother John; on the evening previous to the funeral my brother Henry and I went to view the open grave, and there, among the debris, found an enormous thigh bone (femur) which had belonged to our huge Uncle John; it was nearly the length of my entire leg, although I was then a well grown lad of fifteen.

My mother, **Jean Fullerton**, on leaving Ballownie in 1851, resided with her son Alexander at Fettercairn, till her death, from paralysis, 21st Feb., 1871, aged 79. She was buried in Stracathro. Her individuality was very marked; a woman of middle height; of a lithe, erect finely moulded figure, which was retained to the last; complexion ruddy, eyes brown, hair reddish fair, a voice like a silver bell; a vivacity, volubility and mobility more French than British; a natural grace of movement when speaking, and a rapid change from grave to gay that would have been a fortune in any actress; her intelligence and impulses were direct and clear; her quick temper leavened with a forgiving and kindly tenderness. Her loving energy and industry on behalf of her children makes her memory to them very blessed.

I have done. I leave the continuation of these Memoirs to a Don of a younger generation. I cannot hope that all Dons will take the same interest in their Family and Ancestors as I do myself; but I would fain believe, that, when I have passed away, kindly Dons will not be wanting, to think kindly of him, who, herein has done his best to rescue from oblivion the memory of worthy and revered Ancestors.

The Fifth Commandment is not the least in the Decalogue.

APPENDIX I.

SCOTTISH SEVENTEENTH CENTURY FARMERS.

As so MANY of our Ancestors had been farmers, including all the earlier Dons, I propose to give a short sketch of the ordinary seventeenth century Scottish farm and farmer, a description which would also equally apply to at least the first half of the eighteenth century. In writing this I draw upon information gathered in a study of the general domestic archæology of Scotland.

The persons and surroundings of our four earlier Ancestors: Alexander (Stracathro), Thomas (Dalbog), James (Blackhall), and Alexander (Ireland and Ballownie), covering a period between 1590 and 1779, or close on two centuries, underwent but little change; for it was only towards the close of the last century that the change in men and things began, which has since absolutely transformed rural Scotland. There was probably much less difference between those four men, than there is between father and son in our own day. In speech, in thought, in dress, in habits, as well as general environment they had been much alike; not that there was no economic advance during two centuries, but only that it was very slow, and on lines involving little organic change.

We are therefore warranted in viewing our four ancestors and their compeers first as chronically poor; for there was then very little capital in the country; but we must next regard them as sturdy, industrious and doggedly independent. They were no doubt strongly tinged with the sombre religious beliefs, and even not free from the depressing superstitions of their time; yet, they were by no means morose; but, as the tales, songs and pawky proverbs of the period amply testify, hearty and convivial in their social relations. They were certainly not ignorant or illiterate as knowledge went; for the grand parish schools of John Knox had already been at work; and the democratic Scottish putpit did not stifle thought.

Their speech was a fluent and forcible dialect of Anglo-Saxon, derived from Northumbrian ancestors; and much nearer the original language in words and inflexions than modern English; while a few Gaelic words and idioms were also in use in the lowlands. They one and all cherished, with deep and passionate interest, the memory of Scottish struggles for national independence, political and religious; to a man they were ultra-Protestant.

The dress of the seventeenth century farmer was as follows: a home spun, side-pocketted coat; lappelled waistcoat; knee breeches; deep-ribbed long stockings; brogues or buckled shoes; blue bonnet with red top knot; large neckerchief; a plaid, or tippet tartan cloak. They of course had an every day and a better suit, but with little difference in style or material. The wives, and women folk generally, wore, for every day, short gowns, wincey petticoats, and cotton or linen mutches; but on Sundays and holidays a braw stuff gown; shawl or cloak; and head gear fastened with a silken ribbon, or snood. Their food was simple, but on the whole sound; and probably in nutritive essentials equal to our own; porridge and brose of oat, bere and pea meal; sowans, bannocks; always with milk and butter; barley broth; green and nettle kail; occasionally, braxy mutton; salmon; and beef of the fatted ox or 'Mart' (so named from being killed at Martinmas) salted down at the beginning of winter.

The festivities connected with the killing of the 'Mart,' at all the larger farms, are within my own recollection—as alluded to in the words of the old song:

'It fell about a Martinmas time,'
'An' a gie time it was then,'
'When our gude-wife gat puddins to mak'
'An' boiled them in the pan.'
'O the barin' o' oor door, weel, weel, weel,'
'The barin, o' oor door weel.'

Tea and coffee were unknown drinks; but in their place, thin ale, 'reaming swats,' and at times 'draps o' whiskey,' guiltless of duty, washed down an extra meal. The Scots, like the French, were ever greater eaters of vegetables than the English; but only in a cooked form; raw vegetables, or salads, are as foreign to the true Scot as the eating of eels—the latter thought to be partaking of the accursed serpent!

But the greatest contrast of all between the old and the modern Scottish farmer is in the surroundings; our forefathers were content with houses mostly built of clay and boulders, and invariably thatched or divotted. I have heard old people speak of 'stane hooses,' and 'sclate hooses,' a distinctive phrase from the time when such were rare in rural districts. Some of the farm houses had attics or garrets; but the great majority were of one story only, with a 'but' and 'ben,' and probably a mid-apartment formed by the furniture. For the houses were not divided by partitions but by great box beds and presses; devoid of paint, but scrupulously scrubbed; the floors were of clay or flags, rarely boarded or carpeted; the windows small and fixtures; the doors opened direct out without passage or porch. Besides the box beds and presses, there were in the 'but' the usual tables, plate rack and aumory, with chairs for the gude man and wife, and stools and forms for others. The 'ben' was rather better furnished.

The lighting in the long winter nights was miserable; darkness made visible among the black rafters, if there was no ceiling, either by a tallow dip that wanted snuffing every few minutes; or an 'oily cruizie,' with rush wick, suspended from the mantle-piece; but these illuminants were generally supplemented by blazing whins and fir roots on the low hearth, which spread a cheery glow that coals never give.

But it must not be supposed such dwellings were either comfortless or unhealthy; the box beds certainly were the latter, but the houses themselves were often cozier and warmer, than modern buildings of stone and slate.

The worst feature of the farm dwelling house, however, was its general insanitary surroundings; byre and stable were often built on to it; and such proximity usually led to the obtrusive and offensive midden being at the very door; so commonly was a dung heap in that position, as to give origin and point to a suggestive proverb, 'Better marry ower the midden than ower the 'muir'; that is, a near neighbour's well-known daughter, than an unknown maiden from afar; a maxim, moreover, full of wisdom, and constantly verified in practical experience. The incongruous proximity of middens, dubs and jaw holes, to a trim garden, fragrant, with flowers, southernwood, thyme and peppermint, was indeed remarkable; for we cannot realize the complete indifference of our ancestors to all we now prize in amenity and sanitation.

The farm steading was as poor and primitive as the farm house, and both in keeping with the farm fields; a farm was made up of an aggregation of patches, broken by moor and bog, unfenced, unsquared, undrained, and often water-logged; proper rotation of crops was impossible; and grain, peas and beans, were grown continuously on a wasteful 'inrig' and 'outrig,' or fallow system. It must be borne in mind that cropping rotation only became possible after the introduction of potatoes, turnips and rye-grass; all of which as field crops date after 1720. The first field potatoes were grown in Scotland in 1734.

And the live stock were as poor as the agriculture; horses, rough, light but hardy; cattle scraggy and hairy; sheep black-faced, wild and fleet as hares; the poor beasts were starved in winter, having nothing to eat but coarse grass and rushes cut from the bogs; and to aggravate their miseries cows were often bled at that period to get blood for black puddings; by spring they were so weak that they had to be half carried out of the byres to grass!

These unflattering pictures, scarcely to be credited, are substantiated by the English naturalist Ray; who visited Scotland about 1660; he was no doubt a somewhat prejudiced, and clearly unsympathetic, but none the less truthful witness; for, at that time the English had all the prejudice of pure unreason against Scotland and the Scots. He, moreover, had come fresh from his own fat Essex, full of its bread, beef, bacon and beer, to spy out the leanness of Scottish land. He records, he found the Scottish farmer 'lazy,' ploughing 'with his cloak on'; that he 'lived in a pitiful cote covered with 'turf, often windowless, and without even a chimney; had neither 'good bread, cheese nor drink; lived chiefly on Kail pottage and 'decorticated barley.' We may take it this sombre description applied chiefly to small farmers in the more backward districts; but was, nevertheless all over broadly true.

Scotland, from the time of the War of Independence (1300), up to the Union (1707), had been harried and wasted by political intrigues and religious dissensions, which prevented the accumulation of wealth, and amelioration of the condition of the people; nor did the country fairly start on the path of progress until after the Rebellion of the 'forty five.'—But these centuries of trial, if preventing economic progress, nevertheless welded the people into one of the most cohesive and self-reliant nationalities in existence ; and fitted them for the great part they have played in the civilization of the world during the past hundred and fifty years. They as a nation waited only for peace and security, to assert power and ability to march in the very van of progress.

The forbidding picture I have drawn of the seventeenth, only the better throws into relief the fair prospect of the end of the nineteenth century. The Scotland of to-day, for its size and numbers undoubtedly presents the greatest commercial and industrial activity in the world : it is now second only to England in proportional accumulated wealth ; its chief cities are among the finest in Europe ; its agriculture is rarely equalled, nowhere excelled ; its farms and farm buildings are models to the world ; its live stock of all kinds are of such quality as to be exported to improve breeds in distant lands ; the produce yield from its best lands, in spite of a doubtful climate, is so high as to equal, if not exceed, even the richest lands in England.

But soil and climate are mere raw materials ; it is the vigour, intelligence and moral characteristics of the inhabitants which determines a country's prosperity ; Scotland need not thus fear for the future, while her sons continue to be in the van of art, literature, arms and science. These thoughts are not misplaced in a history of the Dons ; who, as a family are Scoti-Scotorum, and have contributed a fair share towards their country's progress and prosperity.

APPENDIX II.

DAVID SIMPSON'S WILL.

HE FOLLOWING curious document was gifted to James Don, Solicitor, Brechin, on 5th Octr. 1881, by Mary Simpson, living in St. David Street; solely on account of its having the autograph of Alexander Don, the first in Ballownie, as witness to the deed. The said signature is in a bold firm hand, in full length, 'Alexander Don.' The Will is that of David Simpson who held a croft upon Ballownie, and was a subtenant; his descendants remained upon the same croft even up to my own day, but left at the same time as the Don's left Ballownie.

The deed is in good preservation, and docketted;

"Last Will and Testament by David Simpson, 1750."

From its curious phraseology it is worth preserving.

"I David Simpson subtenant in Balewnie in the parish of 'Strickathrow being at present diseased in body But blessed be God 'Sound and perfect in mind memory and judgment And con- 'sidering the certainty of Death with the great uncertainty of the 'time place and manner thereof Doe therefore for preventing all 'Debates & Controversies that might otherwise happen to arise 'after my death amongst my Children after named about the 'division of my worldly means and Effects Make my Last Will and 'Testament in manner following And I Doe nominate make Con- 'stitute and Appoint James Simpson subtenant in Balewnie my 'youngest Lawful Son (under burden of payment of the Legacies to 'my other Children after mentioned) to be my sole Executor 'Legator and universal Intromitter with my whole goods gear Debts 'and Sums of money outsight and insight plenishing of whatsoever 'kind species or denomination the same be of presently pertaining or 'belonging or due and addebted or that shall happen to pertain &

'belong or be due addebted and resting to me the time of my death
'by whatsoever person or persones by Bond Bill tickett and pro-
'misary note or any other manner of way With full power to my
'said Excr. immediately after my death to medle and intromitt with
'use and Dispose off And if need be Call and persue for the goods
'gear Debts and Sums of money aforesaid Compare transact &
'agree thereanent accquittances & Discharges to grant And generally
'every other thing needfull concerning the promises to doe which
'my sole Excr. & universall Intromittar by the Laws of Scotland in
'Such cases may doe And I Legate and bequeath & Will & ordain
'my said Excr. within the space of Twelve months next after my
'death To Conkent and Pay to my other Children after named their
'Heirs Excrs. assignes the respective Sums of Scott's money after
'mentioned Vizt. To William Simpson my Eldest Lawfull Son if he
'is in Life & shall return to this Kingdom within the said space of
'Twelve months & failling of his so returning to this part of the
'Kingdom within sd. space to David Simpson his only Child the
'sum of six pounds To David Simpson my Second Lawfull Son the
'sum of Fourty five pounds To Mary Simpson my Daughter Spouse
'to William Gillespie Cotter in Leuchland the like Sum of Fourty five
'pounds The sum of Fifteen pounds Scotts due by the said William
'Gillespie to me being always allowed & accounted in part of the
'said Legacy to his wife with the ordinary @ rent of the said sums
'after the time of payment thereof while payment according to Law
'Also I Legate & bequeath & Will & ordain my said Excr. immedi-
'ately after my death to Deliver to the said David Simpson my Son
'Two pairs of Bed blankets a single wearing plaid & an old Chest
'And Also immediately after my death I Will & ordain him to
'Deliver To the said Mary Simpson my Daughter Two pairs Bed
'blankets & her mother's wearing plaid & Chest which are in my
'Custody which I Legate and bequeath to Her And lastly I Legate
'& bequeath & Will & ordain my said Excr. immediately after my
'death to Deliver to William Gibson my Grandchild my whole best
'suit of wearing Cloathes & I ordain my said Excr. to pay my
'funerall charges & just & Lawfull debts And Declare this to be my
'Last Will derrogatory of all former if any be which I hereby declare
'void In Witness whereof I have Subscribed these presents con-
'sisting of this & the preceeding page (written by John Spence

' younger Clerk of Brechin) Att Inchbear of Balewnie the fifteenth
' Day of November one thousand seven hundred and Fifty years
' before these Witnesses Alexander Don tennant in Balewnie &
' Alexander Watt in Inchbear of Smiddyhill.'

" De mandato Dicti Davillis Simpson scribere referentis ut
' Aperuit Ego Joannes Spence notarius Publicus hauc et precen-
' dentum pagninam pro illo subjerito'   John Spence N.P."

It would be curious to know what fee John Spence got for drafting this mass of legal subtlety and turgid verbiage, with its absence of stops and strange capitals, seeing that the total cash bequests were less than £10 in our money, and the value of the goods perhaps a bare £10 more, or £20 in all!

APPENDIX III.

THE VALENTINES, LAIRDS OF PITGARVIE, MEARNS.

AM INDEBTED to my cousin, Walter Denham, for the following Genealogical account, and some notes, concerning his and my ancestors on the mother side. The Valentines were clearly an old family in the Mearns; but the absence of Register records, only enables our branch to be traced back to the middle of the seventeenth century. The name is probably of French or Flemish origin, and is fairly numerous in mid east Scotland. It is sometimes spelt Valentine, or Vallentine, and occasionally Wallentine. How our ancestors became possessed of the ancient estate of Pitgarvie, we do not know; although we know full well of the shady proceedings connected with its loss. The first of the recorded names is:

Robert Valentine, 1640 to 1690.

NOTE.—He is described as of 'Wester' Pitgarvie, in some old documents; his wife's name is not recorded.

On 10th July, 1690, his son **David**, was 'retoured' heir to his father Robert, in the estate of Wester Pitgarvie. (Inq. Gen. 7,042).

David 1665 to —

Married **Isobel Pitcairn**, about 1698, and had the following children:—

(1) **David,** 1699 to 1748.
(2) **Elizabeth,** 24th Jany. 1701 to —
(3) **Jean,** 5th April 1703 to —
(4) **Margaret,** 3rd March 1706 to —
(5) **Isobel,** 6th Jany. 1707 to —
(6) **Anne,** 20th Feby. 1710 to —
(7) **Mary,** 4th Feby. 1713 to —

These women are not to be traced; but,

(1) **David**, 1699 to 1748.

Married 7th Dec. 1727, **Jean Fullerton** daughter of Robert Fullerton, in Mill of Conveth, (ancient name of Laurencekirk) and Jean Webster his wife, and had issue:

    (1) **John** (Baptized) 29th April 1729 to 11th June 1767.
    (2) **Alexander** 27th Decr. 1730 to —
    (3) **Margaret** 14th Decr. 1732 to —

NOTE.—The Laird David, was taken up in Montrose, with his tutor, or guardian, in 1716, as a suspected Jacobite; but released after a short confinement. This apprehension, was of course, in connection with Marr's Rebellion in 1715; for the Valentines were Episcopalians, and, if not active, covert adherents of the Stuarts. It is to be noted that David's wife was a Fullerton, and that another alliance with the same name and family took place in the succeeding generation.

(1) **John** 1729 to 1767.

Married 23rd Decr. 1752, **Katherine Crocat**, daughter of John Crocat, Merchant, Fettercairn, and Jean Lindsay, his wife; they had issue:

    (1) **Mary** 1753 to 1850.
    (2) **Alexander** 17th May 1755 to —
    (3) **Jean** 1st Dec. 1759 to —
    (4) **Margaret** 9th Aug. 1761 to —
    (5) **John** 25th Sep. 1763 to —
    (6) **Elizabeth** 19th July 1765 to —
    (7) **David** 6th Aug. 1767 to — (posthumous).

NOTE.—John died and was buried at Marykirk 11th June 1767, aged 38; not 35, as stated in the Register. His initials, with those of his wife, are entwined in monogram fashion, on the lintel stone of the front door in the existing house of Pitgarvie.

John's wife's father, John Crocat, was a well-to-do merchant in Fettercairn; somewhat scrubby, and famed for the careful way he guided his gear; which characteristic induced a wag to scribble on his tombstone,
    "Here lies John Crocat"
    "Wi his keys in his pocket."

All John's children were baptized by the Revd. Alexander Lunan, Episcopal Minister at Luthermuir; who was of course a suspect

Jacobite (like John himself), and, for some years after the rebellion of 1745, was consequently under political and ecclesiastic disabilities. Mary, (my grandmother) coming on the scene shortly after the rebellion, had to be baptized by the said Lunan, surreptitiously; and the rite was carried out in the open air, in a wood in the Glen of Drumtochty; several miles from Pitgarvie. This is a unique tale, in so far that there are probably no other men but ourselves now living in Scotland, who can tell a similar story of their grandmother and the Stuart Rebellion. But the ban against the spiritual functions of episcopal clergymen was soon thereafter removed; for Alexander John and David of the Pitgarvie family were baptized at Mr. Lunan's house, Rosehill, Inglismaldie, and Jean, Margaret and Elizabeth in the house of Pitgarvie itself; which indicates that up to 1767, there was no available Episcopal church or chapel in the neighbourhood. The only married member of John's family was Mary—(of whom hereafter)—and I do not know the history of the others except Alexander and Margaret; the latter was a curious and eccentric woman, who survived till about 1830; and was known in my mother's family as 'Auntie Meggie.' John was succeeded in Pitgarvie by;

(2) **Alexander**, 1755 to 1810.

He died in Montrose, unmarried: with him the estate passed to Sir Alexander Ramsay Irvine, of Balmain.

NOTE.—In 1784, there was a forced sale of Pitgarvie, which resulted in protracted litigation, between Alexander Valentine and Sir A. Ramsay Irvine; because, as I have heard, of some shady gambling transactions. The lawsuit was carried from the Court of Session to the House of Lords; and on 4th March, 1793, was finally decided in favour of Valentine, or rather of his Trustees. Nevertheless, the property passed away. The case is fully reported in the Law Records, and the remarks of the Judges on Sir Alexander Ramsay Irvine's conduct in the business are particularly strong.

(1) **Mary**, 1753 to 1850.

Married 26th July 1788, **James Fullerton**, farmer, Brathinch, Menmuir, (See Appendix IV.), and had issue,

        (1) **Alexander**, 12th May 1789—died boyhood.
        (2) **Jean**, 9th May 1792 to 21st February 1871.
        (3) **Margaret**, 13th April 1794 to 30th June 1839.
        (4) **Katherine**, 15th May 1796—died young.
        (5) **Mary**, 8th February 1798 to April 1858.
        (6) **Anne**, 25th July 1801 to 17th October 1876.

(2) **Jean,** 1792 to 1871.

My own dear mother. Married **Alexander Don.** (Table IX.)

(3) **Margaret,** 1794 to 1839.

Married, about 1828, **Walter Denham,** of Dundee, and had issue :
- (1) **George.**
- (2) **James.**
- (3) **Elizabeth.**
- (4) **Maria.**
- (5) **Walter.**
- (6) **Jean Ann.**
- (7) **Ada.**

(5) **Mary,** 1798 to 1858.

Married, 1837, **Andrew Henderson,** Brechin, and had issue :
- (1) **John,** 1839 to —
- (2) **James,** 1841 to 1863.

(6) **Anne,** 1801 to 1876.

Married, **George Ross,** Brechin, and had issue :
- (1) **Georgiana.**
- (2) **Alexander.**
- (3) **James.**
- (4) **William.**
- (5) **John.**
- (6) **Patricia.**
- (7) **Jane Anne.** (Table XII.)

(1) **Mary,** 1753 to 1850.

NOTE.—Was in many respects a remarkable woman ; first, she was the eldest daughter of an undoubted Jacobite laird, who only saved his estate by prudently committing no direct overt act in the rebellion of '45 ; secondly, she was christened under political and ecclesiastic disabilities, which we now contemplate with wonder ; thirdly, she lived to be almost a centenarian, and to the last retaining her episcopal and Jacobite principles; fourthly, she was the writer's grandmother, who, nearly a century and a half after her birth, is in lively and youthful mood inditing her memoirs ! She was the only real live Jacobite I ever saw. She was intensely conservative in all her ways. When driven, in a phaeton, to see the then (1848) wonder of a locomotive on the new Brechin railway, eyed it well, puffing along, and then said : ' Drive me hame, siccan a thing's no for me.'

She was a particular friend of Dean Ramsay (a Brechin man) in whose famous 'Scottish Reminiscences,' although not mentioned by name, several of her quaint stories figure.

Her appearance and ways greatly impressed me as a boy; and I can never forget my kind Granny; who gave me jam, treacle and sugar ' pieces,' not to mention occasional sixpences ; she took snuff, was rather grim, with large features, and angular body. To the very last she retained the dress, style and speech of a previous century ; her mode of address was of the time of Fielding, more forcible than what we in these mincing days would deem polite ; when, as a small boy, I entered her parlour, she would say, ' Aye, are ye there else, Willie, my cock ? ' which meant : Are you there, nevertheless, my hearty.

Among her many friends, was a tippling Writer in Brechin, who, when in his cups—which was not infrequent—delighted to visit Granny, at the Gallow Hill, Brechin, partly with the object of teasing her, and partly to get a ' dram.' Imagine her on one side, and he on the other of the fireplace: ' Fat brings you here Mr. D.?' she asks; 'I've come to pray wi ye,' he replies; 'Gae awa ye drucken body' she rejoins; then he flops on his knees, but carefully out of reach of her staff, and begins ; ' Have mercy on ' the terrible auld sinner in yon chair ; may her muckle nose ' (it was a twisted member) 'which looketh eastward be turned westward, and the gaudy red-top-knot on her mutch be turned to some decenter ' colour.' By this time Granny and her stick was on him, and he got up, consenting to go if he got a dram, which he knew would be forthcoming from a handy cupboard.

About two years before her death she fell out of bed, and fractured the neck of her thigh bone, which never united ; and, lying disabled, shrivelled to a mummy, which was her condition when I last saw her, shortly before her death, in Jany. 1850. She was buried beside her husband, and his ancestors, in the ancient and long-disused Churchyard of Pert.

APPENDIX IV.

THE FULLERTONS OF ANGUS AND MEARNS.

ACCORDING to the elaborate researches of my cousin Walter Denham, our ancestors, the Fullertons, are believed to be descended from the Fullertons 'of that Ilk' in Ayrshire; although they may be a separate family. The earliest mention of the Fullerton Family, is, in a Charter by the High Steward of Scotland, dated Thursday before the Feast of St. Barnabas, June, 1240; granting the lands of Fullerton, in the Barony of Kyle, Ayrshire, to Sir Adam de Fullerton, son of Reginald de Fullerton. The Carmelite, or Whitefriars Convent at Irvine, was founded by the Fullertons before 1285; and a century afterwards 1399, Reginald Fullerton of that Ilk, entered into a contract with the said Convent of Whitefriars, that for certain money gifts they were for all time coming to pray weekly for the souls of the donor, and his wife, and their ancestors. On 20th Novr., 1307, King Robert the Bruce, granted a Charter to Fergus Fitz-Louis, otherwise Fullerton, of the lands of Kirkmichael, in Arran; from the name Fitz-Louis, Sir Walter Scott considered the family to be of French origin.

The Fullertons, appeared in Forfarshire in 1327; and again the friendship of The Bruce is shown in granting to Geoffrey of Foullertowne, and Agnes his wife, the lands of Foullertoune, in Maryton parish, with the office of King's Falconer in the Shire of Forfar, etc. The keeping of the Royal Hawks was an office of honor and profit in the middle ages, and bestowed only upon families of honorable origin and lineage. Our Scottish Monarchs kept up hawking establishments in different parts of the country; and this one, near Montrose, was evidently simply known as the Fowler's Town; from whence no doubt, the surname originated. That the persons entrusted with the care of the Falcons were of French origin there can be little doubt, as France was the early and greatest centre of the sport of falconry.

The head of the Fullertons in Angus is Henry Alexander Fullerton Lindsay Carnegie, of Kinblethmont, who is a lineal descendant of Geoffrey de Fullerton.

The names Lindsay and Carnegie have of course been assumed through intermarriage.

It will be noticed that David Valentine of Pitgarvie married a Jean Fullerton; while subsequently a James Fullerton married Mary Valentine of Pitgarvie; and these latter were my grandfather and grandmother.

James Fullerton, farmer, Brathinch, Menmuir, was born at the Mains of Kirkton hill, Mearns, 9th Decr. 1747; and died 1815. His father was farmer there; and is recorded as James Foulerton (*sic*); his wife's name was Margaret Christie.

NOTE.—My grandfather, James Fullerton, was a little, fair complexioned, active, intelligent and very quick-tempered man. He was very fond of astronomy, and an ardent student of the heavens; a good story is told of him in this connection: he complained to his laird that the farm was over rented, but was met by the waggish rejoinder, 'James, my man, gin ye wad look mair to the earth, and less to the heavens, your farm wadna be a bit ower dear'!

FINIS.

www.ingramcontent.com/pod-product-compliance
Lightning Source LLC
Chambersburg PA
CBHW022143160426
43197CB00009B/1407